BUDDHISM AND THE MYTHOLOGY OF EVIL

Other books on Buddhism published by Oneworld:

Buddhist Texts through the Ages, trans. and ed. Edward Conze, I. B. Horner, David Snellgrove and Arthur Waley, ISBN 1-85168-107-8

The Gospel of Buddha, Paul Carus, ISBN 1-85168-026-8

A Short History of Buddhism, Edward Conze, ISBN 1-85168-066-7

What the Buddha Taught, Walpola Sri Rahula, ISBN 1-85168-142-6

Buddhism & the Mythology of Evil

A Study in Theravāda Buddhism

T. O. Ling

ONEWORLD
OXFORD

BUDDHISM AND THE MYTHOLOGY OF EVIL

Oneworld Publications
(Sales and Editorial)
185 Banbury Road
Oxford OX2 7AR, England

Oneworld Publications
(U.S. Marketing Office)
PO Box 830, 21 Broadway
Rockport, MA 01966
U.S.A

First published 1962 by George Allen & Unwin Ltd

A CIP record of this book is available from the British Library

ISBN 1-85168-132-9

Cover design by Peter Maguire
Printed and bound by
WSOY, Finland

CONTENTS

Appendix: 96
Survey of the References to Māra the Evil One contained in the Pāli Canon

ACKNOWLEDGEMENTS

I wish to acknowledge the large amount of help which I have received from others in the preparation of this work. I am greatly indebted to Professor H. D. Lewis, of King's College, London University, whose kind encouragement and practical advice made possible the publishing of this study, and who was always ready to give generously of his time in personal discussion. I am glad to acknowledge how much I have benefited also from discussions with Professor Ninian Smart, now of the University of Birmingham, and Dr David Friedman, Reader in Indian Philosophy at the School of Oriental and African Studies, London University. Dr P. S. Jaini, Lecturer in Pali at the School of Oriental and African Studies, guided my researches in Buddhist canonical literature, and especially in the Abhidhamma, and without his guidance I should often have gone astray. The extent to which I, like other modern students of Buddhism, am indebted to the writings and lectures of Dr Edward Conze is very considerable. The Venerable U Nārada Mahāthera, of the Patthana Kyaung in Rangoon, very kindly read through Chapter 2 and made several useful comments and suggestions. At every stage my work was greatly facilitated by the speed and accuracy with which Mrs E. W. Garland and Miss P. Currie produced the typescript.

Finally, I should like to express belated thanks to the Revd Dr John Marsh, Principal of Mansfield College, Oxford, who taught me, some years ago, to see the value of painstaking lexicographical study, and to whom I owe a great deal in the method adopted in this and my previous book.

I hope I have already conveyed to my wife how much I owe to her sympathy and help; I should like to acknowledge it publicly.

T. L.

University Estate
Rangoon, Burma

INTRODUCTION

THE mythology of evil is as manifold as it is universal. A sense of life's evil seems to have haunted men from the earliest times, and has found expression in a wide variety of popular beliefs. The general theme of this book is the relationship that is capable of existing between such popular beliefs, which belong properly to the realm of folk-lore, and the special insights of a radical religion of salvation.

Stated in these terms it is evident that this is a relationship which is capable of existing in other religions besides Buddhism. Popular forms of belief may vary in their details from place to place and from century to century; the superstitions of ancient India may differ in some superficial respects from the superstitions of modern Europe; but beneath the differing forms there are certain basically similar attitudes to the world, and a basically similar understanding (or misunderstanding) of human existence.

Moreover, when Buddhism is described as a radical religion of salvation it is evident that in these terms Christianity, among others, is a comparable system. In the course of the following pages a justification of this way of describing Buddhism will be offered; from the vantage point thus established it will be possible to see how both Buddhism and Christianity differ profoundly from that understanding of human existence which is presupposed in popular beliefs. Moreover, in view of the way in which Buddhism has succeeded in dealing with the relationship between its own essential doctrines and popular indigenous forms of belief and practice, especially in Burma, it is possible that there are here some lessons to be learnt which may prove valuable in other religious situations of a similar nature.

Therefore, although this is primarily a study in Theravāda Buddhism, it is hoped that it will have some value as a contribution to the study of religion in the wider sense. It is based largely upon the evidence of the Pāli canon. This is not on account of any historical priority which this particular corpus of the Buddhist scriptures might be thought to possess (since scholarly opinion is now inclined to give as much weight, if not more, to the Mahāyāna documents in this respect), but solely because, by an historical accident, the scriptures of Buddhism have been more completely preserved in the Pāli tradition. While this will mean that the picture of Māra, the Evil One, for instance, is largely the version found in Theravāda Buddhism, nevertheless the aim will be to draw no conclusions that are inconsistent with the portrait of Māra found in Mahāyāna Buddhism, but only those which may justifiably be said to be representative of Buddhism as a whole.

So far as Western religion is concerned there is a special value in considering an illustration in the field of religious mythology provided by Buddhism, for the latter has no direct family connexions with Judaism, Christianity and Islam. It is a system which starts from quite different presuppositions, and which yet exhibits in practice some features which are strikingly similar to certain aspects of these Western religions. While there seem, as Professor Zaehner has pointed out, to be no common elements between the Judaism of the Old Testament and the more primitive forms of Buddhism,[1] yet in the subsequent history of these two traditions there are some remarkable parallels. The testimony of Buddhism regarding the kind of relations which a radical religion may have with popular indigenous forms of belief will therefore be the more valuable because it is the testimony of an independent tradition.

It is sometimes said of the Buddhism of South Asia that it is nothing more than a thin veneer covering deep rooted and strongly held belief in demons, and that the animism is the genuine religion of these lands. The verdict of W. A. Graham, for example, on the religion of Thailand is that Buddhism is only the official religion—'little more among the country people than a top veneer, which the least calamity rubs off, exposing the immemorial animist beneath it.'[2] On the other hand, the same writer records the very effective resistance which the people of Siam offered to the seventeenth-century attempt on the parts of Arab merchants to convert the country to Islam. He adds that the religious tolerance shown by the Siamese should not be misinterpreted as indifference towards their own religion, but rather taken as evidence of the 'certainty in the minds of the people that no religion can compare with Buddhism as they know it.'[3] From this it would appear that the Buddhism of Siam is after all more than a 'top veneer'.

The same kind of criticism has been made of Burmese Buddhism. In his article on Animism in Burma in the *Encyclopaedia of Religion and Ethics*, Sir R. C. Temple, who was Deputy Commissioner in Burma from 1888 to 1894, begins by saying that it is 'a recognized fact that, whatever the profession of faith may be, the practical everyday religion of the whole of the Burmese peoples is Animism'.[4] Such a judgment has become the basis for successive statements of the same kind by writers on comparative religion; thus in 1945 Dr A. C. Bouquet's verdict on the Buddhism of Ceylon and Burma was that 'any one who knows these countries is well aware that the real faith of their peoples is not Hīnayāna but a thinly veiled animism.'[5]

This kind of view has been challenged by Professor Slater, in his book, *Paradox and Nirvana*. These statements, he says, 'merely reflect, without further evidence or critical examination, an opinion expressed by a European official in a Census Report of 1891.'[6] This opinion, emphasized ten years later by another official was that 'the Burman has added to his Animism just so much Buddhism as suits him. . . .' The survival of animistic ideas among the Burmese is not to be gainsaid, Slater agrees, but after a careful and thorough examination of the matter he concludes that one must hesitate before describing the Buddhism of the Burmese as only a veneer. He quotes an opinion based upon a full inquiry on the subject to the effect that 'Buddhism in Burma has kept itself remarkably free from the practice of taking ideas and customs associated with primitive religion in general and Nat worship in particular and making them its own'.[7] Professor J. B. Pratt's verdict is very similar.[8] The conclusion from this drawn by Professor Slater is the opposite to that stated by the Census Report: 'it is nearer the truth to say that (the Burman) has added to his Buddhism just so much animism as suits his Buddhism'.[9]

In the view of an anthropologist who has recently made a special study of Buddhism in Burma it is misleading and incorrect to think in terms of a rigid dichotomy between what is popular and what is monastic; rather, he maintains, one should think in terms of a continuum, from animistic ideas on the one hand, to abstract analyses of the Dhamma on the other. He describes the religious situation in Burma by saying: 'Previous attempts to define the nature of Burmese religion have been bedevilled by the use of two terms "animism" and "Buddhism" . . . textual scholars saw Burmese religion as a "pure" Buddhism hampered at every turn by animistic practices of partly local, partly Hindu origin.'[10] He grants that if only village and monastic life are studied (separately), 'there does appear to be an inexplicable gap between the worship of a host of varied spirits on the one hand, and the practice of an austere, godless, self-renouncing philosophy or way of life on the other.' Beneath the surface, however, it is possible to discern that there are connecting links between these two, so that, in fact, Buddhism is in living contact with the popular religion; the two are seen 'in their right perspectives as two poles of a continuum which is Burmese religion.'[11] It is with one of these 'connecting links' that the present study is mainly concerned: the important example of a connecting link which is provided by the Buddhist conception of Māra the Evil Onc. It is suggested here that this is one of the important means by which the continuum has been held together, one of the means by which the radical insights of Buddhism have been able to remain in living and fertile contact with popular indigenous beliefs, so that the frontier between Buddhism and popular belief has remained open, but has been firmly controlled from the Buddhist side.

The consideration of such matters will not appeal to the adherents of other faiths who are convinced that they have nothing to learn from the study of religions, and are confident that their own houses are perfectly in order. But for others it is hoped that the material here brought together may not only provoke thought but may also prove in some way illuminating to their own situation.

NOTES

1. R. C. Zaehner: *At Sundry Times* (London, 1958), p. 15 f.
2. *Siam* (2 vols, London, 1924), Vol. 2., p. 292.
3. *op cit.*, p. 294.
4. *E.R.E.* Vol. 3, p. 21.
5. *Comparative Religion* (Penguin Books, London, 1945), p. 129.
6. R. H. Slater, *Paradox and Nirvana* (Chicago, 1951), p. 14.
7. R. F. Spear, *The Syncretism of Animism and Buddhism in Burma* (unpublished thesis), quoted by Slater, *op cit.*, p. 20.
8. *The Pilgrimage of Buddhism* (New York, 1928), p. 127.
9. Slater *op cit.*, p. 20.
10. E. M. Mendelson, art., Religion and Authority in Modern Burma, in *The World Today*, Mar. 1960 p. 115.
11. *op cit.*, p. 116.

1

POPULAR MYTHOLOGIES OF EVIL

Popular demonology in ancient India

THERE is a story, found more than once in the Buddhist scriptures, of a monk, who, contrary to the usual custom, went out at night on an alms-round. A village woman, catching sight of this silent figure, clad in rag robes and carrying a skull as an alms-bowl, standing in the darkness outside her house, uttered a scream of horror: 'How terrible for me!', she cried, 'There's a demon after me!'[1] The intention of this tale, as it stands in the scriptures, is to justify certain regulations which were imposed on monks in connection with the collection of alms. But it also reveals incidentally how natural it was for the ordinary householder of India in the time of the Buddha to interpret an uncanny or frightful experience by reference to the idea of a demon.

It was against such a background of popular beliefs that Buddhism developed. It is a background which can be reconstructed in some detail from evidence found in both Buddhist and non-Buddhist sources. The canonical scriptures of Buddhism, while they are primarily intended to set out the doctrine of the Buddha, also afford some interesting sidelights on the beliefs and practices of the people of India in the sixth century BC. Spirit beliefs are found in association with Buddhism from the very beginning.[2]. Non-Buddhist evidence of these beliefs is available in the Vedic literature, particularly in the collection of hymns and charms known as the Atharva Veda. From these two sources, Buddhist and non-Buddhist, a picture emerges of a world of popular belief peopled by all kinds of spirit-beings, many of whom are demonic, and who in many ways resemble the demons, ogres, goblins and the like, which have held a large place in the beliefs of men of many parts of the world.

In the story just mentioned the word used for demon is *pisāca*. The pisācas, together with the *yakkhas* and the *rakkhasas*, are the most common demons both of the Buddhist Pāli canon and of the Atharva Veda (Sanskrit, *piśācas*, *yakṣas* and *rakṣas*). They are not at all clearly differentiated, their characteristics overlap, and the terms themselves are interchangeable.

There are many allusions to demons in the Jātaka stories, which comprise the most popular section of Buddhist literature and have from the earliest days held a prominent place in Buddhism as a medium of popular instruction. These stories embody a good deal of non-Buddhist material, drawn from the folk-lore of India, and for this reason it is not surprising that they provide a rich source of popular demonology. The first Jātaka tells the story of a caravan of travellers who set out to cross a wilderness beset by demons. These, it is said, come out at night from their stronghold to kill men and oxen and to devour their flesh, leaving only the skeletons beside the road to tell the tale to subsequent travellers. The party in this story travels in two halves. The leader of the first half is very credulous, and is easily deceived by a demon who appears in the guise of a waggoner, approaching from the opposite direction. The leader of the second half is wiser, and not so easily deceived. He and his party, encountering the same demon, notice his red eyes, his aggressive bearing and the fact that he casts no shadow. This last feature marks him and his company out conclusively as non-human creatures, and the travellers exclaim: 'These are not men but yakkhas! They will return in the hope of devouring us!'[4]

A number of characteristic features of these demonic beings are exemplified in this story. They are more often than not creatures whose home is in wild, lonely places. They are more active during the night. They are non-human, often with horrific or uncanny qualities; a yakkha of the forest who seized the princess Sambulā is described as 'with seven tufts inspiring dread alarm'.[5] Another yakkha is described as a kind of hairy ogre;[6] they are often represented as assuming disguises in order to deceive men.[7] They are usually regarded as carnivorous, but most commonly they devour men rather than animals. The Jātakas testify fairly frequently to this idea; they tell of a demon who devoured all who went down into a certain pool, and who were unable to give the right answer to a question he put to them;[8] of a yakkha-town inhabited by female yakkhas who used to entice shipwrecked men, and then imprison and devour them;[9] of yakkhas in a forest whose custom it was to put down poisoned food in the road for unwary travellers to eat; when the travellers had eaten and died, the yakkhas would come out and devour them;[10] of a woman's rival who, reborn as a female yakkha sought to devour the woman's child.[11] These and many other such references, both in Buddhist and Vedic texts, suggest that flesh-eating was the predominant characteristic of the demons.[12]

What their flesh-eating habit denotes is by no means clear. Some scholars have thought that belief in man-eating demons originated among people who had encountered cannibals. The word *pisāca,* which has been noted as one of the common terms for demons, is also known to have been the name of a certain tribe inhabiting the north-west of India, among whom cannibalism is fairly certainly proven.[13] But the question whether these human cannibals inherited their name from the ancient belief in carnivorous demons, or whether it was the other way about, is still unsettled. In general, it seems more likely that the name belonged originally to the demons.[14] Moreover, there is, in the Vedic texts especially, a strong association between the demons and various kinds of sickness. They are responsible for disability of the joints,[15] excessive discharges from the body,[16] insanity,[17] various wounds,[18] and barrenness among women.[19] In the Vinaya Piṭaka the example is quoted of a certain place which some monks had made their residence for the rainy season, but which was then found to be haunted by demons (pisācas), who took possession of the monks and sapped their vitality. This was regarded as sufficient justification for the suspension of the rule under which monks were obliged to remain in the same place throughout the rainy season.[20]

It is thus possible that the idea of demons as 'flesh-devourers' may have had its roots in the connection they had with disease and debility. On the other hand, the fact that in the Atharva Veda they are said to arise in throngs at night-time, the time of their greatest power, and appear to constitute a threat to cows, horses and domestic animals, suggests that they were thought of as mysterious and dreadful creatures of the darkness, somewhat akin to beasts of prey. It has to be remembered that the line between demonic beings and animals was somewhat indistinctly drawn by the people among whom such beliefs were held.[21]

The horrific qualities of the demons were further exhibited by the loud noises which they were thought to make in order to frighten people, especially at night.[22] The story is told of how the Buddha was once deep in meditation, in the darkness of the night, when a demon, coming upon him there, and wishing to make him feel 'dread, horror and creeping of the flesh', raised a great hullabaloo, like a loud and dreadful goat-cry. The similarity between demons and wild creatures with strange cries, such as owls, is attested in the Vedic literature.[23]

The instances which have been mentioned are only a few of many references of this kind which are to be found in the Buddhist suttas and the Vedic hymns, but they are enough to indicate the general tenor of such references. It is evident that the demons of ancient Indian belief represented a fairly wide range of human experience of whatever was dark or terrible. They were the conceptions used in order to explain the mysterious and menacing aspects of men's existence. As A. A. Macdonell wrote in connection with Vedic mythology, such beliefs 'have their source in the attempt of the human mind, in a primitive and unscientific age, to explain the various forces and phenomena of nature with which man is confronted. They represent in fact the conjectural science of a primitive mental condition.[24] Disease of body or mind, the mysterious and dimly understood forces of nature, the hostile forces of the jungle, of deep waters and great mountains, indeed, anything in man's environment that was uncanny or frightening, these were the matters which popular demonology sought to explain, and, to a limited extent, to deal with.

The method of dealing with these hostile forces often, at the popular level, took the form of magic or sorcery. This is the kind of method which the Atharva Veda reflects; it is probably for this reason that these hymns were only grudgingly accepted by the guardians of the Vedic tradition as a part of the Vedas.[25] M. Bloomfield, commenting on the significance of the Atharva hymns and charms, writes: 'the broad current of popular religion and superstition has infiltrated itself through numberless channels into the higher religion that is presented by the Brahman priests, and it may be presumed that the priests were neither able to cleanse their own religious belief from the mass of folk-belief with which it was surrounded, nor is it at all likely that they found it in their interest to do so.'[26] These words are of double interest in connexion with the present study. They are a reminder of the deeply popular nature of the beliefs which are being considered, and they serve also to emphasize the difference between, on the one hand Brahmanism's relation with popular belief, and on the other hand, that of Buddhism and the same popular beliefs—a relationship which is to be examined in subsequent chapters. At this point it is worth noting that the Brahman priests appear to have come to a virtual acquiescence in popular belief; this is to some extent true of Buddhism also, but only when important qualifications have been made. First, however, there is more to be said concerning the popular practices which were connected with demon-beliefs.

Measures for dealing with the demonic

The simplest and most elementary of these was, wherever possible, to keep out of the demons' way. A certain lonely island was regarded by voyagers as likely to be the haunt of demons, and therefore to be avoided, according to a Jātaka story.[27] Before building a house it was apparently the custom to ascertain whether the site was haunted by spirits or not, and the craft by which this was done was known as *vatthuvijjā*; it is a practice which is several times mentioned in the Buddhist Canon, where it is condemned as a low art.[28] Allied with this was the craft known as *bhūta-vijjā*, the knowledge of how to deal with demons.[29]. Those who found themselves the victims of attack from demons would withdraw from the infested place, as did the monks mentioned in the Vinaya. Once the demons had done their evil work, however, the ill had to be countered, often by means of charms. Such charms, directed against disease-demons, form a large part of the Atharva Veda collection. From this it is only a short step to the offering of sacrifices to propitiate the demons. There is good evidence of such practices in the India of the Buddha's time. The word yakkha, which is one of the commonest terms for a demon, is explained by the Pāli Buddhist commentators as being derived from the root *yaj*, to sacrifice, so that a yakkha is understood as a being to whom sacrifice is offered. The etymology may be unsound, but it indicates that there was some connection between yakkhas and sacrifice in common practice.[30] The Jātakas contain several direct references to sacrificial offerings made to demons.[31]

Such, apparently, were the everyday methods by which the people of India sought to deal with the evil results that attended encounters with demonic beings.

These kinds of beliefs and practices are characteristic not only of Buddhism's birth-place, but also of the neighbouring lands of South-East Asia to which Buddhism subsequently spread. Although nowadays animism is said to be slowly giving place to modern materialistic ways of thought, nevertheless so far as the less sophisticated inhabitants of the Theravāda countries are concerned, the same is still very largely true, and has been throughout the past centuries. The nature of these popular beliefs in the lands of Theravāda Buddhism may be briefly noted, in order that their essential similarity to ancient Indian patterns of popular demonology may be seen.

Popular demonology in Ceylon, Burma and Thailand.

Strong and tenacious beliefs in malevolent demons who are regarded as the cause of the many ills of life is well attested among the people of Ceylon. The beliefs of the Vaeddas, the aboriginal people of Ceylon, were collected by Mr Hugh Nevill, and published in 1886.[32] Prominent among them was a belief in malevolent beings called Yakās: 'They cause the various ills that afflict the Vaeddas, and their position is exactly the same as that of the evil spirits whom the Sinhalese denominate *Yakās*. Sickness or misfortune of every kind is attributed to them; but some of them also exhibit their spite by throwing down rocks from the cliffs when people are passing by, and frightening them in the night by strange cries and noises.' From early times down to the present day such notions are found in the folk-stories of the villages.[33] Sir J. E. Tennant, writing in 1859, noted that beneath the surface of Sinhalese Buddhism there burn 'the unextinguished fires of another and darker superstition'. This writer added that Yakkha worship was essentially indigenous in Ceylon.[34]

With regard to Burma the picture is very similar. Deep-rooted belief in Nats, or spirits, has already been mentioned as and outstanding characteristic of Burmese religion. In their hostile aspect Nats exhibit features which are very similar to those of the yakkhas. They haunt woods and lonely places, and even the bravest men hesitate to trespass upon their precincts. Those who do are likely to have their bare bones flung out upon the road as their only memorial, according to a story recounted by Fielding Hall.[35] The thunder of falling rocks in mountainous places, cries and lamentations also witness to the presence of the Nats. A similar account is provided by Shway Zoe.[36] He calls belief in the Nats 'the old geniolatry', and notes that it still retains a firm hold on the minds of the people. He too mentions the grievous injuries which the Nats can cause, their violent attacks, their terrifying nature, and their responsibility for illness.[37] In Burma, says Niharranjan Ray, 'Buddhism gave to the people a religion that replaced the gross and primitive heathenism of earlier centuries.'[38]

In Thailand indigenous beliefs of the same kind are found. Here the evil spirits are known as *Phi*. These, writes an authority on Thailand, are the spirits whose origins are to be found in 'the dark and distant ages before the development of simple animism into that widespread polytheistic religion of which Brahmanism was one branch, and who still inspire the only manifestations of religion amongst the . . . hill tribes of Siam and Further India generally'[39] To describe at all fully the different kinds of evil spirits that vex the lives of the Thai people would require many volumes, he adds. They cause sickness; they delight in leading travellers into the clutches of wild beasts; they cause sudden darkness in which people lose their way and fall over precipices or encounter other grave accidents; some female *phis* are said to allure men and then devour them. The malignant spirits are said to be much more numerous and more venerated in Thailand than are the good spirits.[40]

The Asura-mythology

In addition to the commonplace demons which have been described so far, there is a more exalted class of evil spirits known as Asuras. In the Pāli Canon these differ from the minor demons in a number of respects. Whereas yakkhas and pisācas are often mentioned singly, the Asuras are almost always referred to collectively, as spirit-hosts, hostile to virtue and all goodness. The exception to this collective form of reference is when an Asura prince (*asurinda*) is mentioned; but even here the collective concept is not far away, for an Asura-prince implies the existence of an Asura-host.

Moreover, associated with the Asuras is the idea of a fall from former glory. This idea is bound up to some extent with the history of the word *asura*, and it may be noted that there has been considerable discussion of this matter. According to A. B. Keith, who has provided a convenient summary of the discussion,[41] the change of meaning from a good connotation to an evil one took place in India; 'since Darmesteter, the theory has prevailed that the change by which Asura became the name of demons in India, while in Iran the Devas became demons, is an internal change of meaning in the two languages, brought about by causes which can be made more or less clear'. But alongside this history of changed linguistic usage is the Asuras' mythological history, in which very clearly they are regarded as having suffered a deterioration. It is not a case here that the *word* had changed its meaning and for that reason had to be applied to a different group of spirits; the popular idea was that the *asuras themselves* had undergone a kind of moral or metaphysical fall. This may possibly be the way in which the mythology retains a memory of the change of meaning of the words, but, whether this is so or not, what matters is the idea that in the Pāli canon these are fallen beings, devas in opposition, or in revolt, or disgrace. This notion is encountered in a number of places in the Canon and in the commentaries. Thus, according to the Saṃyutta Nikāya, it was the asuras who first attacked the devas [42] but in the Kulāvaka Jātaka Sakka, lord of devas, is described as resenting the presence of these asuras in the heaven of the Thirty-Three, and therefore intoxicating them and expelling them while they were incapable of resistance. The tradition that asuras had a common origin with devas is attested in another way in the Saṃyutta-Nikāya, where Sakka refers to the asuras as the 'older Devas'.[43]

It is important to notice that in the Canon the asuras are almost always mentioned in conjunction with the devas. An exception appears to be found in the idea of the asura-world as one of the four possible evil destinies (*apāya* or *duggati*—e.g. It 92). But here also the contrast with the devas is implied, in that there are other (good) destinies (*sugati*), and among these is the deva-loka. Apart from this type of example asuras and devas are usually mentioned together. Indeed, the Sakka-Saṃyutta might equally well be called the Devāsura-Saṃyutta. The asuras are usually described as in conflict with the devas, or disputing with them, or possibly intermingled with them.[44] This characteristic of the asuras, their inseparability from the devas, is a feature to which there is nothing corresponding in the mythology of minor demons. Although there are evil yakkhas and good yakkhas, the mention of one kind does not inevitably entail the mention of the other in quite the same way as with the asuras and devas.

The most frequent allusions to asuras occur in connection with their war with the devas. References to this conflict are characterized by the introduction, 'long ago. . . .'[45] This primeval conflict is mentioned in the four Nikāyas, and in various of the books of the Khuddaka Nikāya.[46] In the Saṃyutta Nikāya a collection of suttas is found which is very largely devoted to this theme of the conflict of the asuras and devas.

Separate sources or forms of the myth may account for the different places of abode of the Asuras which are mentioned. According to the Udāna and the Aṇguttara Nikāya[47] they are said to be *ocean-dwellers*, together with various sea-monsters, nāgas and gandhabbas. On the other hand they are said in the Saṃyutta and Aṇguttara Nikāyas to be *dwellers in a city*.[48] These asura-hosts have various leaders or *asurindas* such as Pahārāda;[49] Rāhu;[50] Vepacitti;[51] Verocana;[52] and Sambara.[53] Of these, Rāhu is also found as a figure of cosmic mythology, the 'seizer' of Candimā and Suriya, the moon and the sun. In this connection he is sometimes referred to simply by names without mention of his being an asurinda.[54] To Buddhaghosa, commenting on these legends, Rāhu is a dragon (gaṇḍaka) What is of significance for the present study is that to men who described the solar and lunar eclipses as Rāhu's seizing of the sun or moon, it is evident that he appeared primarily as a dangerous and fearsome being. This may serve to explain how Rāhu came later to be identified as an asura, when asuras were regarded as beings of a hostile, evil nature, the agents of much that was unpleasant or threatening in human experience.

These beings come, more obviously than the commonplace demons, within the realm of religious belief. The asura-mythology, with its theme of conflict with the devas, who are the representatives of virtue and blessing, implies a moral judgment between the devas as righteous (*dhammikā*) and the asuras as unrighteous (*adhammikā*).[55]

Thus in the stage of their development which is represented in the Canon the Asuras, as the opponents of the devas, stand for forces that are in opposition to all that is virtuous, and whose hosts increase with the increase of evil-doing among men.[56] The nature of the relationship between the size of the asura-kāya and the extent of human wickedness is not stated in the passage of the Aṅguttara Nikāya which refers to this idea. It is possibly linked with the idea that rebirth as an asura is one of man's four possible evil destinies (*apāyā*), in that an increase in the number of evil-doers among men would automatically, through rebirth, produce an increase in the number of the members of the Asura-assembly.

Asuras appear also in the Atharva Veda, where they are among the most frequently mentioned demonic beings. In a minority of cases in Bloomfield's edition of the AV (2 out of 19), the word occurs in the singular, namely, as a title for Indra (VI. 8^{3}), and for Varuna (I. 10^{1}). Apart from these all other references are to Asuras collectively, in their role as the opponents of the devas. As in the Pāli Canon, the conflict is usually regarded as one of great antiquity: 'of yore, in the beginning, the gods drove out the Asuras' (IV. 19^{4}); 'the earth upon which, of old . . . the gods overcame the Asuras (XII. 1^{5}) (see also XI. 10^{16}). Frequently Indra (=Sakka, Pāli Canon) is spoken of as the overthrower of the Asuras (II. $27^{2,3}$); (VIII. 5^{5}; X. 3^{11}; XI. 5^{7}). The Asuras appear sometimes as the attackers, as in the Canon: "The devas warded off the onslaughts of the Asuras day after day' (X. 3^{2}, see also X. 6^{22}).

Apart from these references to the primeval conflict, the Asuras sometimes appear to be inhabitants of the earth; they are connected particularly with subterranean activities; they are represented as hiding deep in the ground the plants which cure diseases (II. 3^{3}; VI. 109^{3}); ants are spoken of as their kinsfolk in VI. 100^{3} (this reference is of interest in connection with the simile in the Kulāvaka Jātaka, where the Asuras, after their ejection from Mt Sineru, are likened to ants climbing up a pillar (J. I. 202)). These references may be taken as indications that the process had already begun, by which originally earth bound demons became subsumed into the company of asuras, until eventually the term asura embraced all the evil spirits.[57]

The asura-mythology is thus a type of belief which is distinguishable from belief in the random activities of separate demons, all of whom operate more or less independently. This random operation of local demons has, in the asura-mythology, given place to the idea of great demon hosts, directed from above, by an asura-lord. Regarded from one perspective the asuras of later Indian mythology may be fallen gods; but from another they consist of all the minor evil spirits of ancient India, the *rakkhasas* and *pisācas*, who have now been taken up into this originally more exalted host which has come near to the earth; all the demons in the later literature have become Asuras, and the process had begun even in late Vedic times. 'The enemies of the gods *par excellence* throughout the Yajurveda, the Atharvaveda, and all the subsequent Vedic literature are beings called Asuras but this connexion can be traced only in the latest parts of the Rigveda and even there but occasionally.'[58] But in the Epics, writes E. Washburn Hopkins, the Asuras 'included all the sinful demons'.[59]

It was mentioned above that the Asuras have a special characteristic which distinguishes them from other Vedic demons: the Asura-mythology is always bound up with the Deva-mythology; one group increases at the expense of the other.

Thus, what may be seen to have happened when the minor demons, the *rakkhasas* and *pisācas*, have been absorbed into the Asura host, is that ideas which in their original form are common to primitive mankind in many parts of the earth have now been taken up into the more developed and specifically *Indian* mythology of good and evil; or possibly, as G. Tucci has described it, the characteristically *Asian* mythology.[60] By this he means a mythology free from Iranian dualism. While it is characterized by opposed forces, these are not eternally moral opposites, such as Iranian dualism knows; it is more a matter of polarity. Moreover, man is not directly involved in this; he is affected only when the balance of these forces is seriously upset. 'Man feels himself not so much a responsible actor as the passive target of invisible powers. He does not presume to take part in the war they wage on one another, he submits to it and by various devices and by cunning or malice he tries to edge his way among the shocks and clashes and contrasts.'[61] These words of Professor Tucci recall the tenth of the Sakka Suttas in the Saṃyutta Nikāya (*Sambara*) in which certain rishis sought protection for themselves from the battle that was raging between the Devas and the Asuras. The same mythology is suggested when Professor Tucci says, 'We have not two worlds each inevitably opposed to the other; the limit between the one and the other is uncertain. . . . In that ceaseless struggle we can perceive a vague longing for balance and harmony . . . this is the inner meaning of the myths.'[62] He then illustrates this theme with examples from ideas and practices found in many parts of Asia. The same characteristic of Indian thought is noted also by Sir Charles Eliot, who writes, 'Just as there is no finality in the exploits of Rāma and Krishna, so Ravaṇa and other monsters do not attain to the dignity of the Devil. In a sense the destructive forces are evil, but when they destroy the world at the end of a Kalpa the result is not the triumph of evil. It is simply winter after autumn, leading to spring and another summer.'[63] M. Eliade goes so far as to say 'Dans l'Inde non seulement il n'existe pas de *conflit* entre le Bien et le Mal, mais il existe même une confusion.'[64]

All this has relevance for the present study in so far as the Asura-Deva mythology represents one possible line of development of that earlier kind of demonology which was characterized by multifarious minor demons. That kind of demonology could, however, develop in other directions, or, to express this more accurately, the attitude to the world which underlies this demonology could itself develop other forms of expression, apart from the kinds that have been noted so far. The cults which, in fact did thus develop, are not immediately recognizable as being akin, in essence, to animists' *ad hoc* methods of dealing with the demonic; but when the basic attitudes which animism and, for example, Brahmanism, presuppose, their fundamental kinship becomes apparent.

The attitude to life manifested in animism

The essence of the animistic attitude to life is that the ills which man experiences are attributed to wholly external forces. These forces, conceived as having an existence separate from his own, he regards as hostile. They must be avoided if possible; this is the kind of response which the asura-deva mythology represents, in which man tries 'to edge his way among the shocks and clashes'. Alternatively, they may be propitiated by sacrifices; this is another type of response; or they may be mastered by the invocation of a stronger power, as in the Vedic hymns; or they may be manipulated to advantage by one who possesses the means or the skill to do so. This last kind of response, the manipulation of hostile forces, is the one characteristic of animistic and other forms of magic. It was in this direction that animism shaded into Brahmanism in a way that is in striking contrast to the Buddhist attitude to what are called the 'low arts'. The object of the Brahmanic sacrifices was *ostensibly* to chain the demons; the real object was an extension of this attitude at a more profound level, namely the manipulation for men's advantage of what were believed to be certain hidden natural forces. This point is brought out in the words of Sylvain Levi: 'Morality finds no place in this system. Sacrifice, which regulates the relation of man to the divinities, is a mechanical act, operating by its own spontaneous energy, and that, hidden in the bosom of nature, is only brought out by the magic art of the priest.'[65] Professor S. Dasgupta makes the same point in a slightly different way, emphasizing the quasi-scientific nature of the process: 'Thus the objects of a sacrifice were fulfilled not by the grace of the gods, but as a natural result of the sacrifice. The performance of the rituals inevitably produced certain mystic or magical results by virtue of which the object desired by the sacrificer was fulfilled in due course like the fulfilment of a natural law in the physical world.'[66]

This principle, of an effectual working of the agent upon his environment for his own desired ends, underlies another method which developed as an alternative to sacrifice in ancient India, the method of *tapas*, self mortification, or more exactly, self-torture. 'It is literally "burning, glow"; and had then (in the Ṛg Veda) already acquired the secondary sense of retirement into solitude in the forest, and the practice there of austerity, bodily self-mortification—not at all with the idea of atonement or penance, but under the impression that self-torture of this kind would bring about magical results. Just as the sacrificer was supposed, by a sort of charm that his priests worked for him in the sacrifice, to compel the gods, and to attain ends he desired, so there was supposed to be a sort of charm in *tapas* by which a man could, through and by himself, attain to mystic and marvellous results.'[67]

In all of these cases attention is focussed on the external world. The desire of the individual, to be released from insecurity, or sickness, or to gain power or riches, or whatever other form the desire may take, is held to be realizable if the external world is dealt with in the right manner: by keeping out of the way of the demons, or propitiating them, or invoking a stronger power; by having the right sacrifice performed in exactly the right way; or by carrying out *tapas* with sufficient severity of will.

In contrast to this is the attitude inculcated by Buddhism, which pays primary attention to the inner disposition of the individual. This is not immediately apparent on the surface of popular Buddhism; it is implied however, in the essential doctrines of Buddhism, and to this subject attention may now be turned.

NOTES

1. *Vinaya* II. 115; cf. *Majjhima-Nikāya* I. 448.
2. See E. Lamotte, *Histoire du Bouddhisme Indien* (Louvain, 1958), p. 761 f.
3. For example, the *yakkha*, Ajakalāpa, also calls himself a *pisāca* (*Udāna* 5). See also *Jātaka* V. 420; and cf. *Itivuttaka* 57 f with *Saṃyutta-Nikāya* IV. 154, etc.
4. Jāt. I. 103; cf. Dīgha-Nikāya II. 344 and Jāt. V. 34.
5. Jāt. V. 91.
6. Jāt. I. 273.
7. See, for example, Jāt. I. 129; VI. 303; IV. 491.
8. Jātaka No. 6.
9. Jātaka II. 128.
10. Jāt. III. 200.
11. Jāt. V. 21.
12. Cf. AV. XII 3^{43}; IV. 36^{3}; VI. 32^{3}; I. $16^{1,3}$.
13. See Art. by Sir G. Grierson, 'Piśāca=Homophagoi', *JRAS*, 1905
14. See A. B. Keith, *Religion and Philosophy of the Vedas* (Cambridge, Mass., 1925), p. 238.
15. AV. II. 9^{1}.
16. AV. II. 3^{6}.
17. AV. VI. 111^{3}.
18. AV. V. $29^{5,16}$.
19. AV. VI. 81^{1}.
20. Vinaya I. 149.
21. cf. Semitic demonology. See E. Langton, *Essentials of Demonology* (London, 1949), Ch. I, especially pp. 3-8.
22. e.g. Ud. 5.
23. e.g. RV. VII. 104.
24. *Vedic Mythology* (Strassburg, 1897), p. 1.
25. See *S.B.E.*, Vol. 42, p. xxix.
26. *ibid.*, p. xlv. f.
27. Jāt. IV. 159.
28. D I. 9; II. 87; S III. 239.
29. D I. 9; cf. Vin III. 84.

30. see P.E.D. under '*yakkha*'
31. Jāt. III. 146; II. 149.
32. see H. Parker, *Ancient Ceylon* (London, 1909), p. 139 f.
33. *ibid.*, p. 7.
34. see *Ceylon: an Account of the Island* (London, 1859), pp. 538 and 541.
35. H. Fielding Hall, *The Soul of a People* (London, 1904), p. 255 f.
36. see *The Burman, his Life and Notions* (London, 1882), pp. 276-289.
37. *ibid.*, p. 282 f.
38. *Theravāda Buddhism in Burma* (Calcutta, 1946), p. 263.
39. W. A. Graham, *Siam* (2 vols., London, 1924) Vol. II p. 281 f.
40. E.R.E. Vol. XI. p. 483.
41. *Religion and Philosophy of the Vedas*, pp. 231 ff.
42. S I. 215.
43. S I. 222.
44. A II. 91.
45. *bhūtapubbaṃ*
46. D II. 285; M I. 253; A IV. 432; S I. 222; IV. 201; V. 447.
47. Ud. 54; A. IV. 200.
48. S I. 221; 225; V. 448; A IV. 432 f.
49. A IV. 200.
50. A II. 17; S I. 50.
51. S I. 50; 220 ff.
52. S I. 225.
53. S I. 227.
54. Sn. 465; 498.
55. S IV. 203, for example.
56. A I. 142.
57. see E. Washburn Hopkins, *Epic Mythology* (Strassburg, 1915), p. 46.
58. A. B. Keith, *Religion and Philosophy of the Vedas*, p. 231.
59. *Epic Mythology* p. 46.
60. Art: 'The Demoniacal in the Far East', *East-West*, Vol. IV, 1953, pp. 4 ff.
61. *ibid.*, p. 5.
62. *ibid.*, p. 7.
63. *HB* Vol. I, p. 337.
64. Art: 'Notes de Démonologie', *Zalmoxis, I* (1938), p. 202 f.
65. *Doctrine du sacrifice chez les Brahmanas* (Paris, 1898), p. 9. quoted by T. W. Rhys Davids, *Buddhist India*, p. 108.
66. *A History of Indian Philosophy*, Vol. I, p. 21 f.
67. T. W. Rhys Davids, *Buddhist India*, p. 109.

2

BUDDHISM WITHOUT MYTHOLOGY

It is a remarkable fact, and one which is fully evident from a survey of the mythological elements found in the Buddhist scriptures, that early Buddhism not only tolerated indigenous beliefs of the kind which have been described, but, as will appear in the next chapter, it went farther than this; from the materials which were readily available, so to speak, it produced its own characteristically and peculiarly Buddhist mythology of evil.

Before a more detailed account is given of this special mythology it is important to pause, and to appreciate to the full the significance of the fact that this should have happened. The fact is none the less remarkable even if it be granted, with Senart and Windisch, that there has never been a Buddhism without mythology, historically speaking. It is remarkable in view of the utterly radical nature of Buddhist doctrine, for it would be difficult to envisage a system which appeared at first sight to be more unfavourable towards the existence of mythological ideas of any kind than the severely rational system of doctrine and practice which constitutes the Dhamma, and by means of which men are pointed to Nirvāṇa.

Buddhist doctrine is sometimes spoken of as though it were a perfectly simple matter about which there can be no possible misunderstanding: in this view it is simply a system of ethics. The criticism is justly levelled against some European students of Buddhism that they are too ready to indulge in their own arbitrary reconstructions of 'essential Buddhism'. The method in this kind of case is to go through the Canon and produce evidence to support some particular theory as to what the theorizer holds to be genuine Buddhism, as opposed, it may be, to what Buddhists hold. If the historical study of Buddhism is to avoid falling into this kind of error, it must proceed from some more reliable criterion of what may, and what may not be taken as essential Buddhist doctrine. Such a criterion may be found in the Abhidhamma. Perhaps the matter may be put best by saying that one is less likely to misinterpret the Dhamma with the guidance of the Abhidhamma than without it. This will become clearer when the relationship of the Abhidhamma to the Dhamma is considered.

The Relation of the Abhidhamma to the Dhamma

The Abhidhamma-piṭaka is sometimes loosely described in general works on Buddhism as the 'philosophical' section of the Canon. Such a description lends itself to misunderstanding. 'The Abhidhamma is not a systematic philosophy, but merely a supplement to the *dhamma*,' wrote Wilhelm Geiger. 'The works belonging to it mostly contain merely detailed elucidations of various topics dealing with ethics, psychology or theory of knowledge which are mentioned in the canon. Its form is throughout scholastic. The themes are schematically classified; they are not properly defined but rather described by multiplying synonyms and they are brought into all possible combinations, considered as they are from the most different points of view.'[1] By Abhidhamma, says E. Lamotte, is to be understood not a sort of 'code' but rather the doctrine, pure and simple, shorn of literary embellishments and details of historical context.[2] He points out also that in form the books of the Abhidhamma stand very close to those suttas of a catechetical nature of which specimens are to be found in the earlier collections, that is, in the Sutta-piṭaka.[3] The Abhidhamma, comments Prof. Murti, is the first attempt to synthesize the teachings of the Buddha.[4]

The Abhidhamma may thus be said to represent Buddhism's own criterion of what in the Sutta-piṭaka may reliably be taken as *essential Buddhist doctrine*, that which in the Suttas is mixed with 'conventional truth', to 'suit the mind of the average man'.[5] As an illustration of this, an example may be quoted from the history of Siam. In the reform of Buddhism in that country at the end of the eighteenth century undertaken by King Mongkut and chief monk, one of the most notable features was the publication by the latter of his Kichanukit ('work explaining things clearly'), in which it is affirmed that 'there emanate from the Buddha only the Four Noble Truths and the *Paramattha*—that is, the substance of the Abhidhamma-piṭaka.'[6] It is therefore obviously desirable to follow the guidance which is available in this body of literature, and make this the standard for distinguishing in the religion of Theravāda countries between those aspects of belief and practice which are strictly Buddhist and those on the other hand which are popular and indigenous (or possibly Hinduistic).

It is equally clearly not within the scope of a study of this kind to embark on a survey of the works which make up the Abhidhamma-piṭaka. A work representative of the Abhidhamma, which for this purpose could be used instead, is Buddhaghosa's Way of Purification (Visuddhimagga), which in a sense presents the conclusion of the Abhidhamma in the Theravāda school. Its title is a valuable reminder of the ultimate intention and purpose of the Abhidhamma literature; it is not in the last resort an exercise in scholastic analysis, or the study of philosophy for its own sake; rather, it deals with a Way, the following of which leads to a Goal. As a modern Buddhist monk has written concerning the Abhidhamma, 'Irrelevant problems that interest mankind but do not tend to one's Deliverance have been deliberately set aside'.[7]

Buddhaghosa's Way of Purification has, however, tended to be replaced by a compendium of the Abhidhamma literature entitled the *Abhidhammattha-saṅgaha*, largely on account of the latter's conciseness.[8] This compendium, says Nyanatiloka, contains a 'very succinct résumé of all the essential doctrines of the Abhidhamma', and he who masters it 'will have grasped the whole substance of the Abhidhamma'.[9] Attention will now be turned, therefore, to a survey of this compendium, which may be taken as a sufficiently adequate treatment of the Abhidhamma for the present purpose.

The Subject-matter and Method of the Abhidhamma

The Abhidhammattha-saṅgaha, which may be more briefly referred to as the Manual, begins with an analysis of consciousness (citta). This takes the form of a catalogue of eighty-nine distinguishable states of consciousness, that is, every possible type that can exist in the three spheres into which Indian thought divided the world, Kāmāvacara, Rūpāvacara and Arūpāvacara, together with the fourth and specifically Buddhist sphere, Nibbāna. (AbhS I. 2).

This comprehensive catalogue of eighty-nine different types

of consciousness represents the whole gamut of human mental conditions, from those of the wildest savage to those of the saint who has entered Nibbāna. First in the list come those states of consciousness which are to be found in the lowest sphere of existence—*Kāmāvacara*, the kind of life which is dominated by the five senses and their objects, a sphere which includes not only human but also non-human creatures such as animals, ghosts and demons (*asuras*), and also some of the lower gods or *devas*. It is therefore not surprising that at the head of the Kāmāvacara list of mental states come twelve types of unwholesome consciousness, which have their roots in varying ways and varying proportions in greed, hate and delusion.[10] These types of consciousness are regarded as actively unwholesome, that is they will produce further unwholesome results in the stream of consciousness. These later, unwholesome types which result from previous states, are called 'resultants'[11] and a list of these also is given. Besides these there are states of consciousness which a creature existing in the Kāmāvacara may experience, and which will not have any further effect on the stream of consciousness; these are known as 'inoperative' states.[12] Finally there are a further twenty-four types of consciousness in Kāmāvacara, known as the 'great types', and all of them wholesome. This completes the list of the fifty-four possible types of consciousness that may be found in the Kāmaphere. S. Z. Aung has pointed out that while the author of the Abhidhammattha-saṇgaha doubtless had the first book of the Abhidhamma-piṭaka, the Dhammasaṇganī, in mind when he composed this part of his Compendium, he did not follow the arrangement adopted in his prototype but began with evil consciousness instead of good. Aung suggests that the reason for this may be found in the fact that evil, in the Huxleyan phrase, 'knocks at the door more loudly than the good'.[13] Such a suggestion agrees well with the Buddhist idea which will be examined in the next chapter, that the Lord of this mortal world in Māra, *the Evil One*.

The same process of analysing and cataloguing all possible states of consciousness is repeated, in similar terms, in respect of the other spheres of existence, Rūpāvacara, Arūpāvacara, and Nibbāna. This however, is still only the beginning of the matter.

The fifty-four possibilities of consciousness in the Kāma-sphere, together with the fifteen in the Rūpa-sphere and the twelve in the Arūpa-sphere, a total of eighty-one, are all analysed yet further in the Manual. Each state of consciousness is qualified in a number of ways, and the different ways in which they are qualified are responsible for the number of *cittas*, or states of consciousness under any one heading. Thus, for example, in the Kāma-sphere there were eight states all characterized by greed; these eight are then distinguished from one another in various combinations of ways. First, according to whether they are characterized by joyful feeling (*somanassasahagataṃ*), or by indifferent feeling (*upekkhāsahagataṃ*). Again, within these categories, distinction is made between states that are associated with error (*diṭṭhigatasampayuttaṃ*) and those that are dissociated from error (*diṭṭhigatavippayuttaṃ*). Finally, each of these is again subdivided into states which are spontaneous (*asaṅkhārikaṃ*) and those which are non-spontaneous (*sasaṅkhārikaṃ*).

This method of progressive sub-division, or breaking down of the groups of *cittas* into individual *cittas* according to their constituent features, is characteristic of the method of Abhidhamma, and applies to all the lists of the states of consciousness that have been given so far. It is even applied to the eight states of consciousness that are possible in Nibbāna, which, together with the eighty-one mentioned, make up the total of eighty-nine possible states of consciousness of every kind.

One feature of these *cittas*, or states of consciousness into which all experience is analysed, must be made clear, namely that such 'states' are not static (to this extent the word state is misleading); rather, such *cittas* are to be regarded as following upon one another in lightning succession, within the stream of consciousness. This happens as the underlying continuum, the *bhavaṅga*, reacts in this way or that to events which impinge upon it, or impressions received from outside.

Allied to consciousness, thus described, are its adjuncts (*cetasikā*). The second section of the Manual is devoted to a description of these, which, together with the *cittas*, comprise a major part of the analytical apparatus by means of which experience, and existence itself, is described. These mental properties, or adjuncts, a full list of which is given, are present in varying numbers and combinations in every one of the possible states of consciousness. An account is given of the many and complex ways in which the *mental properties* are related to the *states of consciousness*. In this way the whole range of human experience is accounted for.

After this the Manual shows us how the various processes of cognition, apperception and mental retention are to be understood in the light of the foregoing analysis. On the same basis the doctrines of karma, rebirth and salvation are also explained in minute and technical detail.

'The Abhidhamma,' says Nyanaponika, 'is not a speculative but a descriptive philosophy', and for the purpose of describing phenomena, 'the Abhidhamma uses two supplementary methods: that of *analysis*, and that of *investigating the relations* (or the conditionality) of things'.[14] It is imperative, he adds, to supplement such analysis (as has been outlined above), 'by the constant awareness of the fact that the 'things' presented by analysis are never isolated, self-contained units, but are conditioned and conditioning. They occur in combinations which are constantly in a process of formation and dissolution'.[15]

This second aspect of the Abhidhamma is reflected more generally in the latter part of the Manual. Section VIII is entitled 'A Compendium of Relations' (Paccaya-Saṇgaha-Vibhaga); Section IX is 'A Compendium of Places and Occasions' (Kammaṭṭhāna-Saṇgaha-Vibhaga), that is, the details and circumstances of meditation. The former of these, Section VIII, sets out two principal schemes, which, says the author, are usually taken in conjunction with each other.[16] The first is the formula of dependent origination (*paṭicca-samuppāda*), and the second is the system of correlation (*paṭṭhāna*). This section of the Manual thus reflects the *relational* method which is characteristic especially of the second and seventh books of the Abhidhamma-piṭaka.

The well-known formula of dependent origination sets forth the whole corpus of evil in human existence in a series of causal relationships. In the version of the formula given here there are twelve stages of relational connections. The list begins with ignorance (*avijjā*); because of the avijjā-relationship, *saṇkhāra* arises (according to the commentary this is here a synonym for *kamma*); because of the saṇkhāra-relationship rebirth-consciousness arises (*viññāṇa*) so the series continues until the last stage is reached—decay, death, sorrow, lamentation, grief and despair. 'Such is the coming to pass of the whole mass of Ill'.[17]

It must be emphasized, however, following Nyanatiloka,

that this formula is not a way of tracing back the nature of Evil to some causeless first principle, namely, *avijjā*. Rather, as he points out, 'it was to show through which causes and conditions suffering comes into being, now and hereafter . . . the Paṭicca-samuppāda is nothing but the teaching of conditionality and interdependence of all the manifold phenomena of existence . . .'[18]

The second relational system, to be set alongside the first is that of paṭṭhāna. Here the manual constitutes a summary of the twenty-four 'relations' given in the *Paṭṭhāna*, the seventh or 'Great Book' of the Abhidhamma-piṭaka, which 'provides a most complete and detailed elucidation of the Paṭicca-samuppāda, though here the phenomena are not arranged according to the twelve links of the Paṭicca-samuppāda, but with reference to the twenty-four paccayas, i.e. conditions or modes of conditionality.'[19]. These relational modes are, for example, the relation of root (*hetu*), contiguity, co-existence, reciprocity, antecedence, consequence and so on. Such relations are capable of occurring in any number of combinations; thus mind may bear six possible relations to mind, five to mind-and-body, one only to body.[20]

The final section of the Manual, it has been noted, deals with places and occasions of meditation, or 'religious exercises'. This well indicates the purpose of the Manual, and of the whole discipline of the Abhidhamma: to point the way to Arahatship, to Emancipation. Its spirit and purpose may be summed up in the words with which this section closes: 'On this wise would he cultivate who would attain the supreme Dual Discipline, if he be fain to enjoy the Doctrine's essence, and its mastery gain.'[21]

This outline of the main features of the Abhidhammattha-saṅgaha has been intended simply to demonstrate the characteristic subject matter and method of the Abhidhamma. This method, it has been noted, consists first of applying to all phenomena a process of relentless analysis. The first stage is the well-known analysis of a 'person' into the five *khandhas* or 'heaps', namely form, feeling, perception, impulses and consciousness. The process of analysis does not rest here, however. A more detailed scheme is a classification of elements arranged as cognitive faculties and their objects—the twelve āyatanas.[22] Yet another is the classification of the elements of existence into eighteen *dhātus*.[23] Once this analytical method has been adopted it is capable of extension ad infinitum. According to the author of the most famous of the Burmese commentaries on the Abhidhammattha-saṇgaha, the Ṭīkā-gyaw, classification under the five khandhas is for those who are quick of intellect, and therefore need but an outline to grasp the doctrine, the āyatana classification is for those of medium ability, and the dhātu classification is for those who are slow and require a detailed exposition before they grasp the method and intention of this kind of analysis of phenomena.[24] The final Theravādin classification is that which is given in the Abhidhammattha-saṇgaha; according to this the whole phenomenal world is capable of analysis into 72 *dhammas*, or elements. These are, the 89 states of consciousness which were listed above, as one item, the 52 mental properties (*cetasikā*), 18 material qualities (*rūpā*), and Nibbāna. On the other hand, the Sarvāstivādin school listed 75 of such *dhammas*.[25] But, as Bhikshu Sangharakshita has pointed out, 'despite divergencies in matters of classification between the various schools, they were unanimous in holding that Wisdom was to be cultivated by learning first how to analyse phenomena into the "realities" of which they were composed, and then how to relate these realities to each other in various ways'.[26] Once again, the second aspect of the method of the Abhidhamma is emphasized—the correlation of the results of the analysis. It is the method which is important, and not that the numerical classification, whichever one be followed, should be rigidly adhered to. 'In practice analysis has to stop at components not really ultimate which then have to be synthesized into relations which are not actually exhaustive.'[27]

Thus it is the principle underlying the Abhidhamma which is ultimately most characteristic of it, rather than the descriptive metaphysical scheme or doctrine of elements, whether Theravādin or Sarvāstivādin. The metaphysical scheme is a means to an end, not an end in itself: 'Abhidharma is the metaphysic of each system with which its other disciplines are intimately connected.'[28] It is possible, however, for this to be overlooked, and for attention to be given too exclusively to the terms used, the apparently unanalysable elements which are set out in the Abhidhamma literature. The difficulty is, as Prof. Murti points out, that in the books of the Abhidhamma-piṭaka 'the underlying general metaphysical principles are hardly stated; they can be elicited only by implication.' This statement is even more true for the non-Buddhist student than for the Buddhist, since he is not involved in the other disciplines which are the indispensable accompaniments of the Abhidhamma. It is important to realize, however, that the Abhidhamma is, in essence, "a polemic against substance',[29] and in this respect it is best understood when it is viewed in the lights of later developments in Buddhist metaphysics, particularly the Śunyatā doctrine of the Mādhyamika system. Prof. Murti has argued that this is the *ultimate* development of Buddhist metaphysics, and is contained in germinal form within the earlier analyses. 'The Mādhyamika system represents the maturity of the critical consciousness within the fold of Buddhism.'[30]

Prof. Murti has provided a masterly description of the essential insights of this system, which he calls the central philosophy of Buddhism, 'Śūnyatā (Doctrine of the Void) is the pivotal concept of Buddhism. The entire Buddhist philosophy turned on this. The earlier realistic phase of Buddhism, with its rejection of substance and uncritical erection of a theory of elements, was clearly a preparation for the fully critical and self-conscious dialectic of Nāgārjuna.'[31] It is a continuous rejection of all false views about the self and the world by a *reductio ad absurdum*. 'The root cause of duḥkha, in the Mādhyamika system, is the indulging in views (dṛṣṭi) or imagination (kalpanā). . . . The real is the indeterminate (śūnya); investing it with a character, determining it as 'this' or 'not-this' is making the Real one sided, partial and unreal. This is unconsciously to negate the real; for all determination is negation. The dialectic then, as the Śūnyatā of dṛṣṭis is the negation of standpoints, which are the initial negation of the real that is essentially indeterminate (nirvikalpa, niṣprapañca). Correctly understood, Śūnyatā is not annihilation, but the negation of negation; it is the conscious correction of an initial unconscious falsification of the real.'[32] It is indeed difficult to convey the sense of a work such as Murti's without some degree of misrepresentation, but the general tenor of his exposition may be gleaned from such passages as these. The fundamentally Buddhist approach to the goal of desirelessness (the state beyond all possibility of pain and bondage) is not by the universalization of the I (ātman)—which was the approach characteristic of the Upaniṣads—but by denying it altogether, by a path of relentless negation.[33] Every aspect of personality is dissolved until nothing remains.

It is important to appreciate how far this process is carried. It is so radical that it appears ultimately to constitute a paradox—the supreme paradox of Buddhism; as Slater was concerned to point out, we are faced with the question 'who is there to die, or who is there to survive? Accepting the positive interpretation of Nibbāna, we seem to be left with the contradiction of a Great Peace to be enjoyed for ever—and nobody to enjoy it!'[34] This is precisely what is affirmed in the Visuddhimagga:

> 'Mere suffering exists, no sufferer is found;
> The deed is, but no doer of the deed is there;
> Nirvāṇa is, but not the man that enters it;
> The Path is, but no traveller on it is seen.'[35]

Complete nihilism is not, however, the whole story, and Slater has drawn attention to the role which paradox plays here, as elsewhere, in the formulation of religious truth. Edward Conze has also drawn attention to this aspect of the matter: 'Though generally Nirvāṇa is kept transcendentally remote and defined only by negations, there are distinct remnants of a more positive concept. . . . Deliverance is then conceived as the gradual purification of this consciousness which finally attains to the summit of the 'Realm of Dharma' (*dharmadhātu*), from which it will no longer fall back.'[36] But it is only with regard to Nirvāṇa that this positive concept may be seen; the way of purification must remain a way of negation, of purging away of avidyā, and all the entangling false constructions which avidyā produces. This is the heart of Buddhist meditation. 'The spiritual potency of the Mādhyamika teachings can re-assert itself only if and when it can be reintegrated with meditational practice,' comments Conze.[37]

It is then, a thoroughly radical approach to phenomena which is the most characteristic feature of Buddhism, according to most Buddhist scholars. It is this which the Abhidhamma, as the essence of the Dhamma, brings out and emphasizes, not, it must be understood, as constituting a speculative philosophical system in itself, but rather *a way of salvation*.

It will therefore be evident that it is not even strictly accurate to speak of Buddhist 'doctrine', if by that word is meant a parcel of notions to be handed on and expounded by one person to another. The word Dhamma, with its many associations, conveys better what Theravāda Buddhism is, at heart; it is the contemplation *and the practice* of the way in which existence may be analysed into *dhammas*; it is the practice of relating everything, not to self, but to Dhamma, that which alone is self-existent. Accounts of Buddhist doctrine by adherents of other faiths, if they fail to make this clear, are to that extent incomplete and unsatisfactory. In a sense, the whole purpose of this chapter has been to draw attention to a sometimes neglected fact, namely this: descriptions of Buddhism in terms only of its four holy truths and its holy eightfold path, which leave the matter there, as though Buddhism were but a system of noble ethics, are merely *anticipatory*, without supplying what they anticipate. A list of the items of the eightfold path is only the beginning of the account; the heart of Buddhism is reached when it is understood as a system of meditation directed towards that which Hīnayānists and Mahāyānists are agreed is the goal, and about which, Dr N. Dutt points out, their texts concur, when they say:

> *Yaḥ pratītyasamutpādam paśyati sa dharmam paśyati,*
> *yo dharmam paśyati so Buddham paśyati*

'He who realizes the causal origination of things sees the Truth, one who sees the Truth sees the Buddha.'[38]

Essential contrast between the naturalistic and the Buddhist attitude

This, then, is the essentially Buddhist path to the overcoming of the experience of evil. It is evident that this radical attitude which is found at the heart of Buddhism is in marked contrast with all 'everyday' ways of viewing life. From the point of view of the Abhidhamma analysis, the 'beings' with which the animist peoples the world (whether they are evil spirits or men), must be matters of delusion. But there is a more significant divergence between Buddhism and animism, and it is with regard to method. The animist's method of dealing with the ills of his existence is to look *outward* upon his world, as it were to peer at phenomena which he but dimly sees and understands, hoping to find effective ways of dealing with the more unpleasant of these phenomena, so that the unpleasantness will cease, or be avoided. Popular demonology is in essence the attempt to project personal patterns upon the world, and to identify certain hostile forces or powers in the world, and to discover how best to deal with *them*, by propitiation, spells, chants, sacrifices and so on.

From such an understanding of the inner nature of animism, and from the understanding of the inner nature of Buddhism which has been gained from the Abhidhamma, it is possible to see that between these two attitudes to life there is little, if any, common ground. Yet, empirically the two attitudes are found often in close connection with each other, and about the actual nature of their relationship to each other there is not infrequently some confusion. To this aspect of the matter the present study now leads, by way of a consideration of the Buddhist symbol of Māra, the Evil One.

NOTES

1. *Pāli Literature and Language* (Calcutta, 1956), p. 22 f.
2. *Histoire du Bouddhisme Indien* (Louvain, 1958), p. 197.
3. *ibid.*, p. 202.
4. T. R. V. Murti, *The Central Philosophy of Buddhism* (London, Allen & Unwin, 1955), p. 56.
5. Nyanatiloka, *Guide through the Abhidhamma-piṭaka* (Colombo, 1957), p. xii.
6. *E.R.E.* Vol. XI. p. 483.
7. Narada Thera: *Abhidhammattha-saṅgaha* Pt. I. (Colombo, 1947), p. iii.
8. See W. M. McGovern, *Buddhist Philosophy*, I. Cosmology (1923), p. 25.
9. Nyanatiloka *op cit.*, p. 2.
10. *lobha, dosa, moha.*
11. *vipākāni.*
12. *kiriyā.*
13. *JPTS*, 1910–12 p. 125 f.
14. *Abhidhamma Studies*, (Colombo, 1949), p. 3.
15. *ibid.*, p. 7.
16. *ubhayaṃ pana vomissitvā papañcanti ācariyā* (AbhS. VIII. 2).
17. *evam etassa kevalassa dukkha-kkhandhassa samudayo hoti* (AbhS. VIII. 2).
18. *Guide through the Abhidhamma-piṭaka*, p. 158 f.
19. *ibid.*, p. 114.
20. AbhS. VIII. 8.
21. AbhS. IX. 13 *Compendium of Philosophy*, p. 219.
22. See: Th. Stcherbatsky, *The Central Conception of Buddhism* (Calcutta, 1923), p. 6.
23. *ibid.*, p. 8.

24. See S. Z. Aung in *JPTS*, 1910–12, p. 116.
25. Stcherbatsky, *op. cit.*, p. 78.
26. *A Survey of Buddhism*, (2nd Edn., Bangalore, 1959), p. 98.
27. *ibid.*, p. 97.
28. T. R. V. Murti, *op. cit.*, p. 66.
29. *ibid.*, p. 70.
30. *ibid.*, p. 76.
31. *ibid.*, p. 58.
32. *ibid.*, p. 271.
33. See Murti, *op. cit.*, p. 19.
34. R. H. Slater, *Paradox and Nirvana*, p. 78. f.
35. Vis. XVI: Nyanatiloka's translation, *Buddhist Dictionary*, p. 99.
36. *The Middle Way*, Vol. XXXIV, No. 1, p. 12.
37. *The Middle Way*, Vol. XXXIV, No. 4, p. 149.
38. *Aspects of Mahāyāna Buddhism and its relation to Hīnayāna* (London, 1930), p. 51, where Pāli and Skt. refs. to support this quotation are given.

3

THE BUDDHIST SYMBOL OF THE EVIL ONE

THE demonology of the Pāli Canon is dominated by the single figure of Māra, the Evil One. Long passages are devoted to teaching about the Evil One, especially in the Majjhima, Aṅguttara and Saṃyutta-Nikāyas. Some of this teaching is given in openly didactic form; elsewhere it occurs in the semi-disguised form of legend, that is, stories of encounters with Māra by the Buddha and his followers. This legendary material nevertheless may be seen to have a didactic import, and it is this material which must now first be brought together and considered.

The principal sources for the Māra legend are: the Padhāna Sutta (Sn); the collection contained in the Māra-Saṃyutta and the Bhikkhunī-Saṃyutta (S); the Māratajjaniya Sutta (M); the Mahāparinibbāna Suttanta (D, A, S, and Ud); and the Mahāvagga of the Vinaya Piṭaka. There are also certain minor references in the Vinaya, and in the Sutta Nipāta and the Jātakas. (The Theragāthā and Therīgāthā are not taken into account at this point, since only the verses are strictly canonical, and these give little, if any, indication of the circumstances, and there is thus practically no legendary material in these collections).

In all these instances the mythological figure of Māra is seen as an important feature in stories which purport to describe episodes in the life of the Buddha and the lives of the early Buddhists. In addition, there are certain passages where Māra appears in what may be called a supra-mundane context, as, for example, in the Mahāsamaya Suttanta (D), the Brahmanimantanika Sutta (M), and sutta 10 of the Nānātitthiya Vagga (S).

The first general comment to be made is upon the *extent* of this material; from this survey alone it is clear that the Pāli Canon is by no means lacking in mythology; even though this may not be so elaborate in its details as that of the Mahāyāna. For it should be noted that this material is not, like the general demonology which has been examined, a peripheral feature of the Dhamma; it is not part of the general background of ancient Indian popular ideas, shared by Buddhist and non-Buddhist alike; on the contrary, this material belongs to what is specifically Buddhist, a fact which should become increasingly clear as the analysis of it proceeds. The verdict of Windisch may be recalled here. 'I agree with Senart in believing that the mythological belongs to the essence of Buddhism, and cannot be separated from it. For even if the historical Buddha was simply an ordinary human being there has probably never been a Buddhism completely devoid of mythology.'[1]

Evidence that this mythological material was present in Buddhist teaching from earliest times is provided by the Sutta Nipāta. In this text, the basically primitive nature of which is generally agreed, there are to be found passages dealing with Māra which are as important and as numerous as those of any other book of the Canon of comparable length. Besides this, there are other passages which contain references to Māra, and which on grounds of language or ideas have the appearance of being relatively early.[2]

Thus not only is the Māra-mythology found throughout the Sutta-Piṭaka; it appears also to have been present throughout the process of its formation.

Māra's emergence from the popular demonology

In order to draw out the religious significance of the figure of Māra within Pāli Buddhism the first point to be made is this: Māra emerges from the background of popular demonology, and has obvious affinities with it. There is no sharp division between the popular yakkha-mythology and the Māra-mythology. Material belonging originally to the former has, without much apparent readjustment, been pressed into the service of the latter. A good example of this is the protective chant found in the Māratajjaniya Sutta, now addressed to Māra.[3]

Some of the characteristics of the popular demons, which were noted in the first chapter, may be recalled here in order to compare them with features of the Māra legend:

Yakkhas	Māra
(1) Yakkhas frequently have a terrifying effect on humans, especially at night, which is the time of their greatest power; this is often achieved by loud noises. (e.g. Ud 5.) (2) They haunt lonely places (Jātakas, *passim*); seeing a samaṇa in meditation are likely to try to disturb him (Ud 5).	(1) and (2) Māra frequently tries to assail the Buddha when he is meditating in the darkness of the night (Māra-Saṃyutta, *passim*). This he often does by trying to frighten him (*bhavaṃ chambitattaṃ lomahamsaṃ uppādetu-kāmo*), and his method is frequently the making of a loud noise (Māra-Saṃyutta II. 1; II. 7; III. 2; Thag. 46, 49).
(3) They are able to move about freely and assume all kinds of shapes. (Jātakas *passim.*)	(3) He assumes various guises and shapes; a ploughman; an old brahman; 'various visible shapes beautiful or ugly' (Māra-Saṃyutta I. 3; II. 9; III. 1).
(4) They often appear to be akin to animals or weird birds (AV XII. 1. 49; RV VII. 104; Jātakas 83; 546; 55.).	(4) Among the forms he assumes are not infrequently those of animals and reptiles, either terrible or vexatious: a king-elephant; a king-snake; a wandering bullock (Māra-Saṃyutta I. 2; I. 6; II. 6).
(5) They are connected with sacrificial rites; and hostile to anyone who would deprive them of their offerings. (J III. 146).	(5) He is the upholder of the traditional forms of religion, and urges the Buddha not to forsake the sacrificial rites (Sn 428), or chides him for doing so (Māra-Saṃyutta I. 1).
(6) They are able to enter into and possess human beings (S I. 208; Jāt. 546).	(6) He is described as entering into or possessing Ānanda, Moggallāna, and brahman householders.

In the Pāli canon Māra is in fact sometimes explicitly referred to as a yakkha.[4] It may be noted as of some interest that in the Mahāvastu also he is called the 'great yakkha'.[5]

What is more significant, however, is that not only in name is Māra a yakkha, but he is also clearly characterized as such by the kind of similarities which have just been listed. Another trait linking Māra with the popular demonology is seen in the occasional ascription to him of the name *Kaṇha*, which, according to the Dīgha-Nikāya, was also the ancient common name for a *pisāca*.[6]

Māra as a specially Buddhist development

This emergence of Māra as the single figure dominating the background of demonological ideas in Pāli Buddhism is the more remarkable in view of the trend of Indian mythology at the time of the rise of Buddhism. In Hebrew demonology, in the centuries immediately before Christ, the tendency was towards a unifying of the evil spirit-hosts under their various princes, and towards a coalescence of these demon-princes. In ancient Indian mythology, however, the tendency appears to have been in the reverse direction, according to A. A. Macdonell. 'The older Ṛg-Vedic notion of the conflict of a single god with a single demon, mainly exemplified by Indra and Vṛta, gradually developed into that of the gods and the Asuras in general being arrayed against each other in two hostile camps.'[7]

In accord with this is the fact which has been pointed out by a number of writers, that no conception equivalent to Māra is to be found elsewhere in Indian mythology. 'Māra, dieu de l'amour, de la mort et du péché, dieu presque aussi grand que Brahmā, l'ennemi du Bouddha, diffère beaucoup de Mrityu et ne lui doit presque rien.' Thus writes L. de la Vallée Poussin.[8] E. J. Thomas notes that the name of Māra as a mythological being is not found outside Buddhism.[9] More important, nothing really equivalent to the concept of Māra is found. As Windisch points out, 'he has become the personification of evil and death and of the whole Saṃsāra, and thus a figure peculiar to Buddhism.'[10] Sir Charles Eliot also refers to this fact. 'No sect of Hinduism personifies the powers of evil in one figure corresponding to Satan, or the Ahriman of Persia. . . . Buddhism having a stronger ethical bias than Hinduism was more conscious of the existence of a Tempter, or a power that makes men sin. This power is personified, but somewhat indistinctly, as Māra . . .

as a personality he seems to have developed entirely within the Buddhist circle, and to be unknown to general Indian mythology.'[11] E. Washburn Hopkins, in his *Epic Mythology*, notes one example of Kāma, the god of desire or love, being identified with death (māra), but he adds that this late identification is Buddhistic.[12] In view of this absence from subsequent Indian demonology of any figure comparable with Māra, his prominence in the Buddhist Canon is all the more remarkable.

Māra in Buddhist experience

The question therefore arises: how is Māra's position of peculiar eminence to be accounted for? The answer has been supplied in general terms by Windisch, when he says, in agreement with Oldenberg, that the Māra legend is in essence most closely connected with the doctrine of the Buddha. 'It is this doctrine which gives Māra's being its unity.'[13] But room for difference of opinion appears to exist upon the question of *how* the Māra legend arose in connexion with the Buddha's doctrine.

Windisch's view is set out briefly as follows, in the statement of conclusions given at the end of his chapter VIII, *Die Stellung der Māralegende*.[14]

1. By his Enlightenment the Buddha has overcome Death and the Saṃsāra in that for him and his adherents, no new life and no dying again follow on death.

2. Even the Buddha himself used a poetical mode of expressing this fact: he apostrophized Death—'You are overcome, O Death!'; he personified it, he spoke of Māra pāpimā (Death the Evil), linking it with the older expressions like Pāpmā Mṛtyuḥ in the Śatapatha-Brāhmana.

3. After the Buddha's death such sayings were taken literally, and were woven into legends. And since the Buddha had often spoken in this way in his teaching, rejections of repeated attacks upon him by Māra were assumed to be meant. This is the standpoint of the Māra-Saṃyutta, (with the exception of the last two suttas) and also of the Bhikkhunī-Saṃyutta.

4. The legend concentrates more and more upon the first part of the Buddha's life. His victory over Māra is taken as a single and final event, and placed *before* the Sambodhi. The mythical personification becomes increasingly realistic as Māra's daughters appear, as in the Māra-Saṃyutta (last two suttas), and the Padhāna Sutta.

5. Out of the original poetical language are produced cruder and cruder mythical conceptions. To the last stage belong Māra's demon army and the Buddha's victory in the Lalitavistara, the Buddhacarita and the Nidānakathā, also the Buddha's apotheosis, in the same works.

At certain points in Windisch's argument it is possible, partly as a result of critical studies in the intervening years, to offer an alternative suggestion, so that an outline of historical development may be seen which is more in keeping with the weight of Buddhist tradition on the subject, that is to say, which gives greater importance than Windisch will allow to a crucial conflict with Māra at the time of the Enlightenment.

An alternative to Windisch's view

This is mainly an alternative to Windisch's opinion that the emergence of the legend is to be connected with the Buddha's sense of the hostility of life's common ills and his own awareness that he had conquered all these, of which Death, the supreme evil (Mṛtyu Pāpmā) was the great archetype. On these grounds Windisch argues that in so far as any real basis of the Māra legend is to be found at all, it is in the Māra suttas of the Saṃyutta-Nikāya, with their descriptions of repeated attacks of Māra, rather than in the idea of a single crucial struggle with the Evil One. For, says Windisch,[15] in a long life, danger, trouble and pain would approach the Buddha often enough, as they do other men, and he would have to be continually overcoming these things. 'If one speaks, however, of a single final victory of the Buddha over Māra, which gave him a serene, unbroken peace throughout a long life, then Buddha has risen to the level of the super-human.'[16]

Windisch's apparent reticence to consider a Buddha who is raised above the level of the ordinary man has to be seen in the context of his criticism of Senart; he is writing with the latter's extremely mythological views of Buddha as a solar myth in his mind, rather than the Buddhists' own exaltation of the founder of their religion. The real point at issue here may be expressed by saying that Windisch found the root of the Māra legend in the experiences described in the *Māra-Saṃyutta*, rather than in the crucial conflict with Māra which is hinted at in the *Padhāna Sutta*.[17]

His judgment of the latter appears to have been prejudiced

by the fact that it stands in some kind of literary relationship to parallel passages in the Lalitavistara, the Buddhacarita and the Mahāvastu. These, in their account of the Buddha's conflict with Māra contain elaborate and somewhat fantastic descriptions of that battle, and were *therefore* regarded by Windisch as belonging to a late (because 'over-developed') form of mythology. This in itself is an unjustified assumption. After referring to the 'grotesque' portrayal of the conflict as it is given in the Lalitavistara, the Buddhacarita and the Nidānakathā of the Jātakas, he concluded that 'we can see the direction taken by the development of the Māra-legend, and therefore the simple stories of the Māra-Saṃyutta, which do not possess these characteristics, on the whole form an older type of legend.' In the course of this development (as he saw it, from the Māra-Saṃyutta type of *simple* stories to the *elaborate* conflict of the Sanskrit versions), the Padhāna Sutta had an intermediate position.[18]

Ingenious though Windisch's argument may be, it is a reflection of the viewpoint of the nineteenth-century Anglo-German school of Buddhistic study, rather than an interpretation of the Buddhist view of Māra the Evil One. A full assessment of the Māra-mythology, as it is found in the Canon, demands a return to the traditional Buddhist view, which assumes the crucial struggle with Māra to have been at the time of the Enlightenment.[19] The following considerations have to be taken into account:

1. There is the theme, running through the Pāli Canon, that it is primarily the Buddha, and beside him, only the Arahats, who can discern Māra at all. This theme is encountered in two principal forms. First, there are the conventional descriptive formulas, which occur regularly throughout the Nikāyas, in which it is assumed that it is by his supernatural knowledge that the Buddha is able to discern the whole world as it really is, with its devas, its Māra and its Brahmā, etc. Examples of this conventional formula occur in each of the Nikāyas.[20] A typical form of it may be quoted from the Dīgha Nikāya: *so imaṃ lokaṃ sadevakaṃ samārakaṃ sabrahmakaṃ sassamaṇa-brāhmaṇiṃ pajaṃ sadevamanussaṃ sayaṃ abhiññā* (D I. 87). What is implicit in this often repeated formula is in some places explicitly stated, as for instance, in the Saṃyutta Nikāya, where a distinction is made between the inability

before, and the ability after the Enlightenment, to discern these cosmic features.[21] It is for this reason that the Buddha is described as 'world-knower' (*lokavidu*), and following the Buddha, the Arahat also.[22] Thus, it is only he who is enlightened who sees, among the 'realities' of the world, that which is called Māra.

The second form of this theme is found in the thoroughly consistent evidence of the Māra-Saṃyutta that only the Buddha recognized the approach of Māra, even though others were present.[23] Bhikkhus are also represented as unaware of Māra's presence, easily deceived by his guises, and needing to be instructed in this matter by the Buddha; after this, they too can perceive Māra's presence. But ordinary people, such as the brahman householders of Pañcasālā, described in the Piṇḍam Sutta (Saṃyutta N.) and the brahman mentioned in the Cullasuka Jāt[24] are quite gullible, and do not recognize Māra's presence, either at the time (when they refused to give alms), or even, as Ānanda did, afterwards. The evidence on this point is clear and consistent: the knowledge of Māra's presence and activities is an element of the Buddha's Enlightenment. It is indeed, as Windisch says, the doctrine of the Buddha which gives Māra's being its unity.

2. The second consideration to be borne in mind is that, *apart from the Padhāna Sutta*, there is no real *conflict* in any of the passages in which Māra appears in the presence of the Buddha. A summary dismissal is not a conflict; and this is what Māra receives on every occasion. The Buddha is throughout represented as entirely unassailable by Māra; he always recognizes Māra the moment the latter appears, and to recognize Māra is to deflate him. '*Jānāti maṃ Bhagavā, jānāti maṃ Sugato!*' is the constantly repeated dismal refrain of Māra in his encounters with the Buddha: 'The Lord knows me! The Righteous One knows me!'

3. What then is to be made of a third major item in the reckoning, namely that of the motif running through the Canon which assumes the Buddha's *conquest* of Māra? This is a form of description of the Buddha that occurs by no means infrequently, and is found in the earliest parts of the Canon. For example, in the Sutta Nipāta, the Buddha's conquest of Māra is referred to by his contemporaries;[25] and he also describes himself as 'Crusher of Māra's army.'[26]

Apart from the Padhāna Sutta there is another passage in the Canon which describes an experience of the Buddha in terms suggestive of real struggle, and that is the Mahāsaccaka-Sutta.[27] This contains an account of the events which occurred in the night of the Enlightenment at Uruvelā, only here the conflict is one which is described not in mythological terms, but in the abstract terms of Buddhist doctrine. The thrice repeated refrain is: 'Ignorance was dispelled, knowledge arose. Darkness was dispelled, light arose. So it is with him who abides vigilant, strenuous and resolute.'[28] Alongside this may be placed words of the Buddha in which he is represented as telling the bhikkhus that only by a great effort can Māra be overcome: 'I consider no power, brethren, so hard to subdue as the power of Māra.'[29]

It will be convenient and helpful at this point to make an excursus in order to consider briefly the other encounters with Māra, by the Buddha and his followers, which are described in various other passages. The Brahmanimantaṇika Sutta (Majjhima-Nikāya) provides a good illustration of the two basic features of Māra as he appears in all the legendary material. First, Māra is depicted as the upholder of false views, that is all views (like those mentioned in this Sutta, voiced by Baka the brahmā), which arise out of *avijjā*. (In this role Māra appears also in the Māra-saṃyutta and the Bhikkhunī-saṃyutta; and in the Nānātitthiya vagga, sutta 10, where he is represented as voicing false views which appear to come from Veṭambari (S I. 65 f). In the second place, he is depicted as seeking to prevent the spread of the Enlightenment into which the Buddha has entered, he opposes the making known of the truth which the Buddha has supernaturally seen; he warns the Buddha not to communicate it to disciples, but to keep it to himself. Māra's opposition to the Enlightened One is manifested again in the Mahāsamaya Suttanta (Dīgha Nikāya), where he appears as the great adversary, hostile to the whole assembly of beings who have gathered in honour of the Buddha. His opposition to the spread of the Enlightenment into which the Buddha has entered is apparent also in the Mahāparinibbāna Suttanta, in the fact that he urges him who has become Buddha to enter at once into Nibbāna.

Other encounters with Māra, on the part of bhikkhus and bhikkhunīs, show that he is thought of as seeking any and every opportunity to destroy the insight which has been gained by those who are disciples of the Buddha. The Bhikkhunī-saṃyutta illustrates the continuous opposition of Māra to the practice of meditation.[30] Always it is when a bhikkhunī sits down to engage in meditation that Māra, aware of this, approaches, and tries to distract her by one means or another. In the case of the venerable Moggallāna, in the Māratajjaniya Sutta,[31] Māra tries to upset him by means of a stomach-ache, but Moggallāna reflecting upon the matter soon recognizes the pain as—Māra!

What these legendary stories appear to emphasize is the Buddhist insight into the fact that there appears to be a 'power' which is opposed to Enlightenment, an enemy who besets the way of all who would enter into that state. This power seeks notoriously to disturb the disciple in his meditation. And always he seeks to prevent knowledge of Enlightenment being communicated to others. With the majority of mankind his work is easy; but against those who threaten to leave his realm his greatest effort is put forth; against those who are Enlightened, he is totally powerless, and all his attempts are folly (*passa Kaṇhassa mandiyaṃ*![32]) It is he who has been defeated when a disciple continues in meditation, or becomes fully enlightened.

The fact that in the Māra legend the emphasis lies heavily upon the Buddha's, rather than anyone else's encounters with the Evil One is not surprising. It is an illustration of where the emphasis naturally lies, throughout the Buddhist scriptures, on the Buddha. In this case it reflects the belief of those who encountered this opposition, that there was One who had overcome it, who had broken through the frontiers of Māra's realm, into the transcendent world. This understanding of the pre-eminence of the Buddha, even with regard to other Arahats, finds expression in the words of a modern Buddhist, Bhikshu Sangharakshita: 'What the genius of one man alone could discover . . . may be understood, once it has been discovered, by all who are possessed of sufficient concentration of mind to follow the steps of a demonstration. It is not merely when we do a thing, but when we do it *for the first time*, that the most formidable obstacles are encountered. We therefore honour the Master, not only as an Arahat, or one by Whom Nirvāṇa has been attained, but as a Buddha, as one Who . . . without a guide breaks through the obstacles which block the road to

Nirvāṇa and throws it open once more to the traffic of humanity.'[33]

The words 'once more' are a reminder of the Buddhist doctrine that there have been many Buddhas before the present one, and that each has exhibited the same characteristic, and has proclaimed the same way, that is, the same Dhamma (for there is only one). Thus, also, each has, in his turn, conquered Māra and transcended his realm. Several passages are found in the Suttas which testify to the conquest of Māra as one of the regular outstanding achievements of a Buddha.[34]

A return may now be made to the main course of the argument. In the light of these considerations it is apparent that, as soon as a religious system had come into existence, a system of emancipation, a system which pointed to an ineffable Nirvāṇa, a system centred round the transcendent figure of the Buddha (and all this is true of Pāli Buddhism, no less than of the Mahāyāna), it was inevitable that the conquest of that power which enthralled men and held them from Nirvāṇa would be attributed first and foremost to him who had opened the way in his own Enlightenment. That is to say, the Buddhist tradition which associates a crucial struggle with Māra with the event of the Sammāsaṃbodhi is inevitable; it could not be otherwise. In spite of Windisch's attempts to reconstruct it from an historical point of view, this is the legend *as it is actually found in Buddhism*. Indeed, if such an association of the Sammāsaṃbodhi with a crucial defeat of Māra were not a feature of the Buddha-legend, then one of two inferences would have to be drawn: either, in view of all that is said of Māra in the Canon, the Enlightenment was not complete enlightenment; or, Māra is not intended to be regarded by Buddhist as the deadly enemy which he is everywhere in the Canon made out to be.

The concensus of evidence in the Canon thus points to these conclusions with regard to Buddha and the Māra legend: (1) in the course of the Enlightenment the Buddha has won a crucial victory: ignorance was dispelled . . . darkness was dispelled . . . (*avijjā vihatā, tamo vihato* .. — M I. 117); (2) being Enlightened, he becomes fully aware of the nature of the opposition against which he has been struggling; (3) to this opposition is given the name of Māra; of Māra it is said that no power is so hard to subdue.

The Padhāna Sutta thus states explicity what is implied in other passages in the Pāli Canon: it projects the Buddhist understanding of the situation into the past, into the story of the Buddha, and the setting, as the Bodhisatta strives 'self-resolute in ardent musing bent', is described in terms of an imminent conflict with the Evil One. The fact that the one involved in this conflict is described in the Pāli canon as Buddha and not Bodhisatta is not a serious objection, and may be taken as an indication that the story is told from the later perspective. That Bodhisatta is meant may be inferred from the Sanskrit versions, which speak of the Bodhisattva at this point in the narrative.

A word may here be added regarding the relation of the Padhāna Sutta to the Sanskrit versions. The fact that the impending crucial struggle, described in the Padhāna Sutta of of the Pāli Canon, is also described in much more elaborate terms in a number of Sanskrit parallels in no way detracts from the orthodoxy of the passage from a Buddhist point of view. Indeed, the very resemblance between the Pāli and the Sanskrit versions at this point may be regarded as an illustration of a principle which is more generally accepted now than perhaps it was in Windisch's day, that one 'must proceed from the assumption that both Pāli and Sanskrit text preserved as a fixed core a very primitive tradition.'[35] Somewhere, apparently, in this primitive tradition, there was a stage at which the Buddhist motif of struggle first found expression, at the mythological level, in the peculiarly Buddhist figure of Māra. From an historical point of view the most that can safely be said is that it was *the Dhamma coming into contact with the popular demonology* that produced the symbol of Māra. In this sense agreement is possible with Windisch's statement that the Māra legend is closely connected with the doctrine of the Buddha.

Once this had happened, however, the Māra legend would begin to grow. For, as A. A. Macdonell pointed out, 'as soon as a person has taken the place of a natural force in the imagination, the poetical fancy begins to weave a web of secondary myth, into which may be introduced in the course of time material that has nothing to do with the original creation, but is borrowed from elsewhere. Primary and essential features, when the material is not too limited, betray themselves by constant iteration.'[36]

The primary features of the Māra symbol, indicated by constant iteration throughout the Suttas, will be considered later in this chapter. But at this point it is interesting to note that the Māra legend illustrates also what Macdonell says about the material borrowed from elsewhere. An example of this is the absorption of Namuci into the figure of Māra.

Namuci was originally a separate demon in Indian mythology, and as such he appears even in the Pāli Canon, in the Mahāsamaya Sutta.[37] In Vedic mythology he was a drought-demon, he who 'withheld the waters'[38]; he was smitten by Indra, thunderbolt in hand, and thus the pent-up rains were released. To an Indian peasant the drought-demon would obviously have appeared as a most malignant being, threatening the welfare, and indeed the life, of the whole countryside—a type of utmost malevolence. In Buddhist demonology this figure of Namuci, with its associations of death-dealing hostility, was taken up and used in order to build up the symbol of Māra; this is what the Evil One is like—he is Namuci, threatening the welfare of mankind. Only Māra does this on a grander scale than the Vedic Namuci, not by withholding the seasonal rains, but by withholding or obscuring the knowledge of truth. The meaning of the name Namuci is given a new significance, which is mentioned explicitly in the commentarial literature; he is Na-muci (*na-muñcati*) in the sense that he does not release (his victims). This easily-heard overtone may well have been another of the reasons for the adoption of the name as a synonym for Māra in Buddhist tradition.

Other figures which have been absorbed into the figure of Māra are indicated by the list of his aliases: besides Namuci he is also known as Kaṇha, Antaka, Pamattabandhu, and Adhipati. It has been pointed by J. Masson that when these names were used in early Buddhist teaching about Māra, the hearers would think first of the demons bearing those names, whose history was familiar to them. That this was so may be inferred from the brief allusions to them and the long passages which follow.[39] But the hearers would not only think of the demons they already knew; they were now hearing them spoken of in a new connexion, they were seeing them in a new light; the demon-symbols were being used in the service of the Buddha-dhamma, and they were to some extent, therefore, being re-interpreted, or given a new content. While this no doubt was the original purpose for the use of these names in connection with the Māra-mythology, their survival in the texts has a value for the historian of religion in providing an indication of the way in which the Māra-symbol grew by absorption of popular demonological material.

THE SYMBOL OF MĀRA IN RELATION TO BUDDHIST DOCTRINE

'The essential features of the symbol betray themselves by constant iteration.' This is certainly true of the symbol of Māra, in the references to him which are to be found throughout the Pāli suttas.

Māra, death and evil. In the first place it may be noted that Māra has obvious affinities with the Brahmanic figure of *Pāpmā Mṛtyuḥ*, Death the Evil One. This, as the primary element in Māra's nature was pointed out by Windisch in his chapter on Māra's origin.[40] 'Māra has *pāpimā* regularly applied as an adjective, and nothing shows him up more clearly as a devil, an evil enemy, than this word,' observes Windisch. He then goes on to show that *pāpimā*, used in this connexion, has a specifically Indian history behind it. In older Sanskrit literature the word is always a masculine noun, with the meaning '(the) ill', disaster, or 'sin'. It indicates, says Windisch, not only moral evil, but also, more objectively, misfortune, sorrow, pain. It is in this last meaning that it is found personified as a masculine deity, similar to Mṛtyu; examples of this usage found in the Atharva Veda and Bṛhadāraṇyaka Up. are given by Windisch. These and similar references he regards as indications that the epithet *pāpimā* referred originally to the fact that death is an evil, an ill.

On the change of form, from *Mṛtyu* to *Māra*, he makes the important observation that whereas Māra's army is referred to as *Maccunasenā*, it is less usual, although not unknown, for the Evil One himself to retain the name Maccu. Etymologically, Māra is closely connected with Maccu (Skt *Mṛtyu*). But the form *Māra* expresses the character of this allegorical-mythical form more intelligibly than *Mṛtyu*, for while Mṛtyu indicates death itself, Māra is a *nomen actoris* to the causative *mārayati*; thus, etymologically, Māra indicates the god who slays, or causes to die.

It is in connexion with death, but particularly the overcoming of death, that Māra is often mentioned in the Canon. In this context death is always regarded as an evil, the unwelcome *Antaka*, the ender of an existence which is not ready to be ended, for the important reason that it has not succeeded in ridding itself of evil.[41] Windisch has made out a case for saying that men's desire for release from repeatedly having to undergo death is older than the desire for release from rebirth. Some traces of this may be reflected in the horrific nature which Māra exhibits, but it is also evident that the sting of death for the contemporaries of the Buddha was that death was regarded as the inevitable precursor of further karmic existence, existence that would therefore be evil and sorrowful. It is for this reason that Māra's realm (*māradheyya*) is equated with 'birth and death', and the fear that is associated with them.[42]

If *pāpmā* stood for the 'ill' of life, then it is evident that death is rightly regarded as the supreme ill, the pāpmā *par excellence*. For in this kind of view death is the event which finalizes beyond any appeal, or possibility of amelioration, the 'ill'-ness of this present existence, even though it be one of a series. Now in the Buddhist description of the situation it is the word *dukkha* which is used for this quality of ill. The holy truth of Ill is that 'Birth is ill, decay is ill, sickness is ill, death is ill . . . '[43] Moreover, in what follows in the statement of this holy truth it is evident that death would constitute the supreme example of dukkha, for 'to be conjoined with what one dislikes . . . , to be disjoined from what one likes, not to get what one wants . . . ', could have no better illustration than death; and since each of these is dukkha, it is evident that death is the extreme of dukkha.

Thus Māra, or Antaka, while he is the mythological heir of Mṛtyu *pāpmā*, whose features he so clearly embodies, is also the mythological approximation to the dark aspect of human existence, which, in terms of the holy truths of Buddhism, is called *dukkha*.

The teaching about Māra which is found in the Canon deals, however, with many other important aspects of the symbol. The didactic material, scattered throughout the Suttas, when gathered together, is capable of simple re-arrangement in accordance with what appear to have been the principal concerns. These may be summarized as follows: *Māra's domain*—or, where Māra operates; *Māra's forces*—or, the agencies of Māra; and finally *Māra's defeat.*

Māra's domain. Where does Māra operate? This is dealt with in the answer to the question asked by Rādha, in the Saṃyutta Nikāya: 'They say Māra! Māra! How far is there a Māra?'[44] In his reply the Buddha indicates where, ontologically, Māra is to be encountered: 'But what is this Māra? Corporeality is Māra: with regard to this Māra you should overcome your longing. Feeling is Māra . . . Perception is Māra . . . Mental formations are Māra . . . Consciousness is Māra . . . with regard to this Māra you should overcome your longing.' Thus, each of the five *khandhas* in turn is declared to be Māra (*rūpa . . . viññāṇa*). Since the five khandhas are 'the five aspects in which the Buddha has summed up all the physical and mental phenomena of existence, and which appear to the ignorant man as his Ego',[45] it will be seen that Māra symbolizes the entire existence of unenlightened humanity.

Another answer to the question, at what level, or in what area of life does Māra operate? is found in the words which are put into Māra's mouth in the Kassaka Sutta: 'Mine, recluse, is the eye, mine are material shapes, mine is the field of visual consciousness. Where can you go, recluse, to escape from me? Precisely mine, recluse, are the ear, sounds, the field of auditory consciousness; the tongue, tastes, the field of gustatory consciousness; the body, touches, the field of tactile consciousness; precisely mine, recluse, is the mind, mine are the mental states, mine is the field of mental consciousness.' All these claims of Māra are conceded by the Buddha: 'Precisely yours, Malign One, is all this. But where there is none of this, there is no coming in for you.'[46] It must be noted that what is claimed by Māra, and conceded by the Buddha as belonging to Māra, includes not only the fivefold group of sense-organs, physical objects and the resultant awarenesses, but also the mind, mental states and mental consciousness.

What emerges from these definitions is a conception of the whole of saṃsāric existence as the realm over which Māra rules: all this is Māra's domain (*Māradheyya*), or Māra's precincts (*Māravisaya*). In terms of Buddhist cosmology this is a way of referring to the whole of life apart from Nibbāna. In the Sutta-Nipāta Māra's domain is said to be very hard to get through (*suduttara*); in the same passage it is likened to an entanglement, strongly stretched out and very deceptive.[47] Sometimes this is called Māra's stream.[48] Only those who are already destined for Nibbāna—the arahat, the anāgāmi, the sakadāgāmi, and the sotāpanna—can cross this stream; they only 'go safely beyond', and by this, the commentary says, is meant 'beyond *saṃsāra* to *nibbāna*.[49] Again, in terms of Buddhist cosmology, this means that Māra's influence is thought of as extending not only over the Kāmaloka; he may also operate in the Rūpa- and Arūpa-lokas. Only in Nibbāna is his influence unknown.

Māra's forces. How does Māra operate? The references found in the Canon provide two kinds of answer to this question; these are not alternatives, but answers given in different terms. Thus, the first answer is one which makes use of mythological terms: Māra behaves like one of the demons of popular thought. He uses deceptions, disguises, and threats, he possesses people, he uses all kinds of horrible phenomena to terrify or cause confusion. Like the demons, who resent interference with the sacrifices,[50] he tries to prevent any attempt to dispense with the sacrificial rites and religious austerities.[51]

The second answer is in the abstract terms of Buddhist doctrine. Frequently associated with Māra's activities, are the evil roots, *rāga, dosa* and *moha,* which sometimes are explicitly mentioned,[52] and sometimes are not mentioned but are clearly implied. In the Theragāthā[53] the bonds of Māra (*Mārabandhanā*) are equated with *rāga, dosa* and *avijjā.* Wrath is described as death's snare[54], and also are the passions.[55] A refrain constantly repeated in the Therīgāthā (hence, presumably a well-established idea) is one which identifies love of pleasure (*nandi*) and thick darkness (*tamokkhandha*) with the power of Māra.[56]

A comprehensive form of expression which is frequently used to cover all these unwholesome moral states is the collective term *Mārasenā*, Māra's army, or Māra's forces. Enumerated in detail in the Suttanipāta these consist of passion, aversion, hunger and thirst, craving, sloth and torpor, fear, doubt, self-will, cant, and various forms of self-exaltation.[57] Prominent among these, and specially closely connected with Māra is the first, passion (*kāma,* or *rāga*).

Such a way of describing 'Māra's army' with the obviously

abstract nature of its constituent forces, is sufficiently transparent not to allow of being mistaken for a host of demonic spirits, and no doubt this transparency was obvious to those who used this figure of speech. Nevertheless, once the analogy has been introduced, it is not surprising to find that there are some references which suggest that Māra is ruler of a host of demons, who partake of his nature. For example, in the Vinaya reference is made to a devatā of the retinue of Māra.[58] Still, this tendency does not appear to have gone very far, at least within the Pāli Canon. In references to Māra's retinue the feature of unmistakable central importance and prominence remains the single figure of Māra. There is no appreciable development of Māra in a pluralistic direction in the Pāli Canon. He remains singular, the Evil One, and in one place at least, the idea is explicitly mentioned and emphasized. 'Even if there were 100,000 seducers like you,' says the bhikkhunī Uppalavaṇṇā to Māra, 'I should not be the least bit excited, so what can you do, by yourself, Māra?'[59]. Even in the Mahāyāna literature, where the idea of Māra's legions is more prominent, the dominant emphasis is still upon the lord of these legions, Māra himself.

Another passage of interest, which provides a further clue to the nature of Māra's agencies, is one containing no direct reference to Māra at all. This is the account of the Buddha's enlightenment found in the Mahāsaccaka Sutta of the Majjhima-Nikāya.[60] It has already been noted that this may with good reason be regarded as evidence about the nature of the opposition which, in Buddhist thought, has been encountered and overcome by the Buddha.[61]

In this Sutta the refrain, three times repeated, emphasizes that it was ignorance and darkness which were dispelled at the Enlightenment of the Buddha. Both these conceptions, ignorance (*avijjā*) and darkness (*tama*), are used prominently in connection with Māra's activities. Thus, the bonds or snares which Māra uses are identified as the three unwholesome roots of action, lobha, dosa and moha.[62]. Of these three, *moha* (or *avijjā*, its synonym), is generally considered the basic member of the group. In the parable of the deer (Mahāsaccaka Su), *avijjā* is the decoy by which the enemy (Māra) leads the deer (mankind) astray into dangerous ground. In the Brahmanimantaṇika Sutta, Māra is represented as having a special interest in encouraging and upholding false views (*idaṃ niccaṃ* etc.), put out by Baka the Brahmā. The Buddha in correcting these false views, tells Baka that they are the outcome of *avijjā.*[63] These examples are sufficient to indicate the close relationship between Māra and *avijjā*. It is instructive to place beside Buddha's words in the Dīgha Nikāya, 'I consider no power so hard to subdue as the power of Māra,'[64] some words found in the Itivuttaka (8) 'I see no other single hindrance such as *avijjā*'. Now *avijjā* (Skr *avidyā*), 'not-knowing', in Buddhist usage has the special meaning of not knowing (or not seeing) things aright, not seeing things as they really are; having one's view distorted; *avijjā* is that which veils 'man's mental eyes . . . preventing him from seeing the true nature of things'.[65] The affinity of thought between this and *tama*, darkness, is obvious and close. Common to both *avijjā* and *tama* is their capacity to blind men. It is instructive therefore to notice that besides ignorance, darkness and blindness are not infrequently associated with Māra's activities. In the Māra-Saṃyutta the approach of the Evil One with the intention of blinding, or confusing the understanding of his victims, becomes a stereotyped formula.[66] Moreover, Māra's connexion with the idea of darkness is attested in one of the commonly used alternative titles applied to him, 'the Dark One' (*Kaṇha*); by his appearance to the Buddha and the bhikkhus as a 'smokiness, a murkiness';[67] by the idea that his hosts are routed as darkness is dispelled by the sun;[68] and by the frequent identifying of thick darkness (*tamokkhandha*) with Māra's power in the Therīgāthā. When all these references are considered synoptically and an outline of the Māra symbol begins to emerge, it is not hard to see that the symbol has been developed particularly where it overlaps these ideas of *avijjā* and *tama*.

It is interesting to recall in this connexion that the *Paṭicca-samuppāda* formula, which has in view the 'whole mass of suffering' inherent in human existence, has usually *avijjā* as its first member.[69]. It was this formula of Dependent Origination which, according to the Vinaya, the Buddha recited, in its forward and reverse directions, at the time of the Enlightenment.[70] It is at this point in the Vinaya narrative that the Buddha describes the experience of *clear vision* which comes to one engaged in ardent meditation as 'the routing of the hosts of Māra.' Thus Māra, basically a symbol of the ill (*pāpmā*, *dukkha*) of existence, or suffering, and closely associated with *avijjā* as the means by which ills are to be accounted for, provides a fairly close approximation in mythological terms, to an early and important element of Buddhist doctrine, the *Paṭicca-samuppāda* formula.

It must also be noted that in the Māra mythology craving (*taṇhā*) is also found closely associated with Māra. *Taṇhā* is a synonym for lobha, and the connection of *lobha, dosa* and *moha* with Māra has already been mentioned.[71] In the Māra-Saṃyutta *Taṇhā* is the first of Māra's three daughters. In this respect, it will be seen that the Māra symbol, which brings together the fact of the evil or suffering of existence and *taṇhā* as the agent of this suffering, provides in mythological terms a parallel to the second Holy Truth, concerning the cause of *dukkha*.

Thus the symbol of Māra the Evil One, embodying as its most prominent features the ills of human existence and their hidden roots, bears a close resemblance to the general shape of early Buddhist doctrine. What differentiates it from these abstract expressions of doctrine are the grotesque features which link it with popular contemporary demonology. It is in this dual nature of the Māra symbol, this relatedness both to Buddhist metaphysics and to ancient Indian demonology, that constitutes its peculiar value, and to this important topic a return will be made later.

Māra's defeat:

By whom is Māra conquered? To this question the answer given in the Canon is, pre-eminently, by the Buddha. This has been sufficiently demonstrated in what was said about the Buddha and Māra in the previous chapter. It is an essential part of his title as Buddha that he is also the '*Mārābhibhū muni*'.[72]

But Māra is also conquered by those who walk in the path of Buddha. This aspect of the matter receives much attention in the Suttas. However, to speak of the conquest of Māra is only one possible form of expression; there are a number of others which suggest that Māra is overpowered, but without any direct encounter or conflict. There is found in the Suttas quite frequently the idea of the *evasion* of Māra, or strategic escape from Māra, when the Evil One has been deluded or deceived by the Buddha's follower.[73] This is seen more clearly when the many separate references to the 'worsting' of Māra (in one way or another), scattered throughout the Suttas, are brought into juxtaposition.

These references may most conveniently be considered by arranging them in order, beginning with those that speak of the overcoming of Māra in very *general* terms, and going on to those which emphasize *more particular* methods by which this is to be accomplished.

How is Māra conquered? It is in the answer to this question that the specially Buddhist nature of the symbol of Māra appears, for the means by which he is conquered are precisely the means of liberation which are emphasized in Buddhism generally. To put this in another way it can be said that if all the passages found in the Canon which refer to the conquest of Māra are brought together and arranged systematically the result will be a fair conspectus of the Buddhist way of salvation.

Sometimes the overcoming of the Evil One is spoken of in broad general terms; in the Theragāthā, for instance, such conquest is attributed to all who are followers of the Buddha or who adopt the Buddha's religion.[74] Sometimes the eightfold path is spoken of as the way of deliverance from Māra.[75]

On other occasions, however, the way of Māra's conquest is specified more exactly. One of the items of the eightfold path the first, right-view (*sammā-diṭṭhi*), and the last three, right-effort (*sammā-vāyāma*), right-mindfulness (*sammā-sati*) and right concentration (*sammā-samādhi*) are specially mentioned as the means of overcoming the Evil One.

Thus, it is said that the bhikkhu who 'sees aright' has conquered Māra and his mount.[76] Again, Māra's realm is said to be transcended by him who regards the world as void and has uprooted all false views about self.[77]

Right-effort, or right striving, (which has to be understood as a striving for enlightenment) is emphasized in the Aṅguttara Nikāya as the means of transcending Māra's realm;[78] they who have developed the four-fold way of striving for enlightenment have overcome Māra's realm. One element of this effort for enlightenment is particularly mentioned; this is the effort to develop the seven factors of enlightenment (bojjhangā), and in a passage in the Saṃyutta Nikāya[79] is the prescribed method of crushing Māra's forces.

Of these seven factors of enlightenment which are part of right-effort, two are mentioned as being specially important where Māra is concerned. These are right-mindfulness and right concentration.

More than one passage in the scriptures is devoted specifically to the importance of mindfulness in connexion with resistance to Māra.[80] The four 'applications of mindfulness' (*sati-paṭṭhāna*) are said to constitute the bhikkhu's own 'proper ground', remaining in which he is safe from the danger of Māra.[81] It must be remembered that mindfulness here is a technical term with strong connexions with the practice of Buddhist meditation. The so-called 'new Burman' method of meditation described by Nyanaponika Thera is in fact the method of mindfulness, or sati-paṭṭhāna.[82]

It is however right-concentration, or *sammā-samādhi*, which more than any other single method is emphasized as the means constituting protection or release from Māra. There are three grades or levels of such concentration; they are usually distinguished as preparatory concentration, approach concentration and attainment concentration. The third of these is the kind of concentration which is held to be present when a person enters into the state technically known as absorption, or *Jhāna*.[83] There are eight *Jhānas*, and together they form the central stages of Buddhist meditation.[84] What is significant for the present study is that the *Jhānas* are specially emphasized in the Canon as a means of overcoming Māra. They are commended as a refuge from Māra,[85] in the parable of the Citadel it is said that the 'good things' which bring comfort and sustain the life of the Citadel against attack (by Māra) are the *Jhānas*.[86] In the parable of the Crops the importance is emphasized of abiding where there is no access for Māra, and this is said to mean abiding in the *Jhānas*.[87] In the Itivuttaka it is said that the overcoming of Māra is for those who delight in the *Jhānas*.[88] These may be taken as representative examples of the frequent association of the practice of absorption or meditation, with the idea of overcoming the Evil One.

Thus, the means by which Māra is conquered coincide very largely with the means by which the central purposes of Buddhism are realized; that is, in general terms, by the following of the eightfold path; in particular, by the practice of meditation. Some words of the Dhammapada express both the general and the particular aspect of the matter, and provide a useful summary of what the Canon as a whole has to say on the subject:

> Those who enter the path, and practise meditation,
> Are released from the bondage of Māra.[89]

Māra and the unitary nature of evil. When considered against the background of contemporary popular Indian demonology what is remarkable about Māra is the degree of integration which this symbol possesses. What previously might have been attributed to a thousand and one different kinds of yakkhas is now all regarded as potentially capable of being explained by reference to this one, ubiquitous, ever-active embodiment of Ill. To some extent this appears to have been anticipated in the Brahmanic Mṛtyuḥ; but in the non-Buddhist mythology there was another related element in the situation, and this was represented separately by the figure of Kāma, the god of passion or desire. In the fully developed form of the Māra symbol in the Buddhist Canon, however, these two have been fused into one, and it is this which constitutes much of the special effectiveness of the symbol. A useful example of the way in which these two elements have been combined is provided by the Mārasaṃyutta. Here, the *names* by which the Evil One is addressed are predominantly coloured by the idea of death (see below p. 120). But it is significant that the *activities* in which the Evil One is engaged are those of Kāma, that is to say, the activities of seeking by various means to distract men from meditating. The lesson which the Mārasaṃyutta points, among others, is this: he who thus *acts*, and seeks to distract men from the path, is desire (Kāma), and his true *name* is destroyer (Māra or Antaka).

Thus the term Māra is not properly understood if it is thought of as having two *alternative* meanings, either of which has to be determined in any given context, so that in one context Māra means the passions, and in another it signifies death. To use the term this way is to destroy its effectiveness. Certainly Māra has two aspects, as Buddhaghosa observed, *maccu* and *kilesa*, and now one, now the other may be predominant; but the two aspects must always be understood as present, or the symbol has no value, and need not have come into use—Mṛtyu and

Kāma could well have been taken into Buddhist mythology unchanged, and have continued to function as separate entities: Māra would be superfluous. Radhakrishnan emphasizes this essentially two-fold aspect in his comment on a verse in the Dhammapada, where he makes clear that Māra is not simply a figure of speech for the passions (as some commentators are inclined to suggest), even though these passions be understood as evil; he is rather, Radhakrishnan says, 'the power for evil that makes for death'.[90] The two aspects of Māra's nature are complementary and both should be always understood.

The monistic nature of this approach to the dark side of human experience introduces a measure of consistency into what otherwise is incoherent and chaotic. Belief in Māra the Evil One as a unity, and all that such belief implies, would, it is evident, afford a man a much more comprehensive understanding of what to the animist would appear as a tangle of blind forces.

It was subsequent scholasticism which divided the Māra symbol into four aspects: the *khandhas*, the *kilesas*, the *devaputta*, and death (see E. J. Thomas, *History of Buddhist Thought*, p. 146 f.). J. J. Jones, in his translation of the Mahāvastu, refers to these four appellations of Māra, and even a fifth (Māra of the *saṃskāras*) added by some commentators, but notes that it is doubtful whether these can be taken as evidence of belief in four Māras. 'The compiler of the *Mhvu* . . . is clearly thinking of only one and the same Māra. He has nowhere a distinct legend of each of the four.' (*The Mahāvastu*. Vol. III, p. 261. n. 3.) Similarly, the daughters of Māra, who appear occasionally, have no independent existence apart from Māra and are regarded in the same light as the constituent forces of Māra's army.

There are certain pragmatic advantages which follow from this unification in the Māra symbol. To adopt a humble analogy, it is as though a man plagued by mosquitoes should first of all try to deal with each one individually as it attacked him; later however it is revealed to him that he can combat them more effectively by taking measures which may appear superficially to be quite unrelated to the immediate nuisance—that is, by going away and suppressing the mosquitoes at their source, and preventing them from breeding. Perhaps the analogy with Buddhistic method would be even closer if the man were thought of as taking regular doses of anti-malarial medicine. In the course of his life he is still exposed, as before, to 'the slings and arrows of outrageous fortune', but because of his larger understanding of the situation, and his preventive action, these can no longer affect him as they did formerly. The measures by means of which the Buddhist understands that the ills of life (its *dukkha* or *pāpmā*) are to be dealt with are, similarly, measures which may appear not to have any relation to the form in which *dukkha* is immediately experienced. For in the Buddhist system the conquest of Māra is achieved not by concentrating on the ills of life and trying to deal with each one as it comes (the method of the animist), but rather by 'seeing things steadily and seeing them whole' and by cleansing the inner existence (*bhavaṇga*) of whatever is likely to produce reactions of an evil kind; this cleansing is achieved by mindfulness and meditation. Thus, the ills of life are *transcended* rather than abolished. What ceases, or is subject to destruction (*nirodha*) is the experience of dukkha, that is, life *experienced* as grievous and sorrowful. By another analogy it may be said that a man showered with bullets will not find security in trying to deflect the bullets one by one as they arrive, but rather by seeing the bullets and the range of fire and the gun from which they are shot as a complex whole, and then, in the light of the knowledge of this whole, taking action of a kind that will place him outside the area of danger. Māra is the mythological symbol to which may be conveniently related various factors of the human situation: the contingent ills of life and the source of those ills are, in the teaching concerning Māra, brought into correlation with one another in a single conception; in the light of this it is possible to discern what kind of action will lead to the transcending of life's ills.

This monistic understanding of the demonic replaces the pluralistic understanding which is offered in popular demonology; the Buddhist analysis of the human situation is in radical contrast with what is implied in animism. Basically the difference is more than one of degree, although superficially this is all that appears at first: Māra is the great yakkha, the yakkha *par excellence*. But fundamentally there is a difference of kind between the view of life reflected in animism and that which the symbol of Māra presupposes. The demons of ancient India are in most essentials closely akin to similar popular conceptions found in many other parts of the world. But this cannot be said of Māra, to whom there are very few real parallels, if any.

The significance of this distinction between the demons of popular thought and Māra may be better understood in the light of a recent discussion of the nature of mental images; 'dominant images, whether they arise from the course our experience takes or from some native propensity to form them, do not by the mere fact of being dominant or being made inevitable for us in some fundamental way, acquire a religious character. They can only be religious when they reflect some religious insight or experience . . . there is nothing in the fact of being innate or very pervasive to establish a proper linkage of any of our images with this religious insight.'[91] In the terms of this discussion of the matter, demons may be seen as 'dominant images', for the forming of which men almost everywhere appear to have a 'native propensity', and some such images appear to be innate, or at least very pervasive. Māra, however, is an image or symbol of a very unusual kind, and it has been one of the purposes of this study to suggest that this is because the Māra-image is the outcome of *a radical religious insight.* Yakkhas and pisācas belong to naturalistic thought, and such conceptions appear to have arisen spontaneously among men everywhere. Māra is not a natural feature of popular thought in this way; he is more properly to be regarded as a 'revelation', a conception due to the insight (*abhiññā*) of the Buddha, for without this insight, there is no knowledge of Māra.

To summarize what it has been the intention of this chapter to show, it may be said that the Māra symbol, as it appears throughout the Canon, is one which, while most of its raw material is taken from the common stock of Indian demonology, is nevertheless a unified conception which takes its shape from the pattern of Buddhist doctrine.

Moreover, it can now be seen more clearly what justification there is for speaking of this figure of Māra the Evil One as a symbol. 'A symbol,' wrote Dr Inge, 'is the representation of some moral or spiritual truth under the form of natural things. Its object is suggestion or insight, it is a kind of language.'[92] To the common people of Buddhist India, yakkhas, rakkhasas, pisācas and the like were, it has been noted, part of the natural scenery of the world. In India and the neighbouring countries these were regular features of folk-lore, just as ogres, goblins, trolls and similar creatures used to be in Europe. Such a creature is Māra, regarded from one point of view—he is a 'natural thing'. But he is also much more than a yakkha. From another point of view his being dissolves into metaphysical abstractions, and one becomes more aware of the moral or spiritual truth of which Māra is also the negative representation. The most prominent single characteristic of the symbol, which appears from whichever point of view he is seen, is the sense of *hostility* which he always conveys. He is a continual reminder of the *dukkha* which adheres in man's existence, and which is concealed beneath the meretricious appeal of all sensory life; he is a reminder also that wisdom consists in taking the necessary steps to ensure the cessation of *dukkha*. In brief, the development of the figure of Māra provides a good example of the process described by J. Wach as characteristic of the early stages of a religious movement: "common religious experience begins to be formulated according to the norms set by the founder . . . simple symbols are designed to express dramatically the same truths which theology wrestles with intellectually.'[93]

NOTES

1. Māra und Buddha (Leipzig, 1895), p. 182.
2. It. 50, for example.
3. See Appendix (pp. 103 ff. below).
4. e.g. in the Sutta-ending '*tato so dummano yakkho* . . .'; see Māratajjaniya-sutta and Godhika-sutta (Mārasaṃyutta).
5. *Mahāntaṃ yakṣaṃ*—Mv. ii. 260. 10; 261. 11.
6. D I. 93.
7. *Vedic Mythology*, p. 156.
8. *Indo-Européens et Indo-Iraniens* (Paris, 1924), p. 312 f.
9. *Life of the Buddha*, p. 217 n. 2
10. *Māra und Buddha*, p. 197.
11. *Hinduism and Buddhism*, Vol. 1.
12. *Op. cit.*, p. 166.
13. *Māra und Buddha*, p. 185.
14. *Op. cit.*, p. 213.
15. *Op. cit.*, p. 210.
16. *Op. cit.*, p. 210.
17. See Appendix (pp. 144 ff., below).
18. *Op. cit.*, p. 204.
19. cf. e.g. Mv. III. 273.
20. See Appendix, pp. 96 ff, 100, 110, 116 f., 139, 141, 143 f. and 160.

21. S II. 170.
22. S. I. 62; V. 197; 343 etc.
23. e.g. Mārasaṃyutta I. 5; I. 9; I. 10; II. 2; II. 4 etc.
24. J III. 494.
25. *Mārābhibhū muni*—Sn. 545; 571; *Mārasenappamaddana*—Sn. 563.
26. *Mārasenappamaddana*—Sn. 561.
27. M. I. 240 ff.
28. E. J. Thomas's translation, *Life*, p. 67 f.
29. D III. 77.
30. See Appendix, pp. 128 f. below.
31. See Appendix, p. 103 below.
32. D II. 261.
33. *A Survey of Buddhism*, p. 42 f.
34. e.g. D. III. 196; Buddhavaṃsa 54.
35. J. J. Jones, *The Mahāvastu*, Vol. II. p. x.
36. *Vedic Mythology*, p. 6.
37. D II. 259.
38. *Na-muñcati.*
39. *Religion Populaire dans le canon bouddhique Pāli* (Louvain, 1942), p. 103.
40. Māra's Ursprung, *op. cit.*
41. On this point see the article by W. Stede, 'Antaka' in *Indian Culture*, XV, pp. 53-56.
42. *jātimaraṇa-bhaya*: A II. 14; see also It. 40; 50.
43. S V. 421; E. Conze's translation, *Buddhist Scriptures* (London 1959), p. 186.
44. S III. 188 ff.
45. Nyanatiloka, *Buddhist Dictionary* (Colombo, 1950), p. 76.
46. S I. 114 f; translation by Miss I. B. Horner, *Buddhist Texts* (Oxford, 1954), p. 107 f.
47. Sn. 357.
48. *pāpimato sota*, e.g. M I. 225 f.
49. M A II. 267.
50. J III. 146.
51. Sn. 428; Māra-Saṃyutta I. 1.
52. e.g. It. 56; 92.
53. Therag. 281.
54. A IV 98.
55. Kāmā: A IV. 357.
56. Therīg. 59; 142; 188; 195; 235.
57. Sn 436-438.
58. Vin III. 69.
59. Therīg, 231.
60. M I. 204 f.
61. See supra p. 53 f.
62. e.g. It 56; 92.
63. M I. 326.
64. D III. 77

65. Nyanatiloka, *Buddhist Dictionary*, p. 24.
66. *vicakkhukammā*, Māra Saṃyutta II. 2; 4; 6; 7; 9; III. 1; 2.
67. S I. 122.
68. Ud. 3.
69. An exception is in D. II 55; where the usual first two links and the fifth are omitted.
70. Vin I. 1[1] f.
71. See above p. 60.
72. See note 25, and D III. 196; and Buddhavaṃsa 54.
73. e.g. Dh 274.
74. *Buddhasāsana*—Therag. 256.
75. Dh. 274; It 50 f.
76. A II. 17.
77. Sn 1118 f.
78. A II. 15 f.
79. Bojjhaṅga-Saṃyutta, Sutta 43.
80. e.g. Ud. 61; M III. 88 ff.
81. S. V. 146 f.
82. See *The Heart of Buddhist Meditation* (Colombo, 1956).
83. See Nyanatiloka, *Buddhist Dictionary*, p. 142.
84. For a general account of the Jhānas see R. N. Smart, *Reasons and Faiths* (London, 1958), pp. 96-101.
85. A IV. 432 f.
86. Nagarūpama Sutta, A IV. 106 ff.
87. M I. 158 f.
88. It. 40.
89. Dh. 276.
90. *The Dhammapada* (London, 1950), p. 60.
91. H. D. Lewis, *Our Experience of God* (London, Allen and Unwin, 1959), p. 142.
92. *Mysticism in Religion* (London, 1949), p. 73
93. *Sociology of Religion* (London, 1947), p. 142.

4

THE SPECIAL VALUE OF THE SYMBOL OF MĀRA

'IT is possible to utilize any means appropriate to the person . . . for leading him to the ultimate truth. There is no limit to the number and nature of the doctrinal devices that may be employed to realize this end.'[1] Such a doctrinal device is the Māra symbol, and it is in this light that the Māra symbol has emerged in the course of the inquiry so far.

Some idea of the prominence of Māra in Theravāda Buddhism may be gained from the frequency with which the theme of the conquest of Māra appears in stone sculptures. Random examples from Burma mentioned by Niharranjan Ray are those excavated at Hmawza,[2] those in the Ānanda temple at Pagan built by King Anawrahta,[3] and various other works in stone recovered at Pagan.[4] In all of these the Māra theme is found. A similar prominence of this theme of Māra's conquest is to be noted in connexion with the statues found in the monasteries, a point which will be dealt with more fully later.

The question now arises: Why did this particular symbol gain such prominence in Buddhism? It has already been noted that the idea of the Evil One is not common in Indian religion generally. Why was it, then, that this became one of Buddhism's doctrinal devices for leading men to the truth? Allied to this question is another: among Buddhists, had it this special value for all alike, or only for a particular section of those who call themselves Buddhists? The answers to these questions will, it is believed, throw some interesting light on Theravāda Buddhism as a religious system.

The Māra symbol—popular or monastic?

A beginning may be made by considering whether the figure of Māra is likely, from the evidence we have, to have been more prominent among laymen than among the bhikkhus, or vice versa.

In the Abhidhamma Piṭaka, both in the matters which are dealt with, and in the manner of dealing with them, one seems to have left far behind all thought of Māra the Evil One. This may be taken as an indication that the Māra symbol belongs to a different level of Buddhist thought, that it is a feature which may well be dispensed with at the more advanced stage of development represented by the Abhidhamma. Now since the Abhidhamma is largely the preoccupation of the monks, the natural conclusion might seem to be that a mythological form such as Māra, graphic and relatively easily comprehended, had value simply and only for the laymen of Theravāda countries. There are indications, however, that this is not the case.

1. The first of these hints is to be found in the Jātakas. This collection of stories of the Buddha's former existences is one of the important media of *popular* instruction in Buddhism. Yet it is remarkable that while minor demons of all kinds are found here as abundantly as anywhere in the Canon, Māra is almost entirely disregarded. In only eight of the 546 stories is his name mentioned. It cannot be said that Māra is deliberately excluded; he is there, but his presence is so slight and unobtrusive in the Jātakas as a whole that the conclusion seems unavoidable that none of those who heard these tales were expected to take him very seriously into account. This is one possible reason for the virtual absence of Māra from the Jātakas, although it must not be pressed too far, since there is another factor to be borne in mind, which partly offsets the weight of this argument. This is that the Jātaka stories consist of materials culled largely from non-Buddhist, pre-Buddhist sources, that is, ancient Indian folklore and legend; the Jātakas, writes N. Dutt are non-Buddhist in character, they 'have nothing to do with the fundamental teachings of Buddhism'.[5] Since Māra is a specially Buddhistic conception his absence from these popular stories is to some degree less remarkable than it otherwise might appear. However, even although Māra would not be likely to appear in the Jātaka proper, that is, the ancient story which is enclosed within the Buddhistic framework, he might conceivably occur as a feature of the framework, had it been felt necessary or advisable to include some teaching about Māra in this material for popular consumption. On balance, therefore, the evidence of the Jātakas suggests that the Māra symbol was

not primarily a popular doctrinal device for laymen. On the other hand, the *Theragāthā* and *Therīgāthā* contain many indications of the place Māra held in the thought of the monks and the nuns. These collections, as Oldenberg commented, are "highly significant for the understanding both of the religious theories and of the religious feeling prevalent among the ancient Buddhist Order.'[6] In the Thera- and Therīgāthā the position of Māra is the reverse of that noted in the Jātakas; here there are more references to the Evil One, and less to the demons. A similar type of literature is found in the Bhikkhu- and Bhikkhunī- Saṃyuttas of the Saṃyutta-Nikāya, and here again the theme of the conquest of Māra through ardent meditation is found frequently. (S II. 277 f; 279; 295; etc.).

2. Another indication pointing in the same direction is found in the monasteries of the Theravāda countries. A common feature of these are the statues of the Buddha which they contain. Each monastery usually has a number of them, showing the Buddha in various attitudes, and one at least is usually given a place of special importance and dignity. The President of the Siam Society in 1913, in a study of the statues of the Buddha found in the monasteries or *wats* of Siam, noted that 'every *Wat* contains the statue of the Buddha . . . those in sitting attitude appear to be the most numerous, and among them again, the temptation of the Buddha by Māra, and the Buddha in self-concentration'.[7] Thus two themes are constantly presented to the inhabitants of the monastery: that of conflict with Māra, and that of meditation.

A fully descriptive account of the statues of the Buddha in one particular monastery has been provided by Prince Damrong Rajanibhab of Siam. This is of special interest because what he describes is not a random accumulation of statues, but a collection made deliberately and with some care. The list begins with the three statues in the Bōt, a place of special importance where ceremonies are performed. Of these three the central one is the *Phra Buddhajīnarāja*—'Buddha seated . . . in the attitude of subduing Māra.' Next are described the two statues in the Sāla in front of the temple. Of these two again, one is a representation of the Buddha 'seated in the attitude of subduing Māra.'[8] There then follows a list of fifty-one statues which stand in the inner gallery, and of these again eighteen are images of the Buddha in the attitude of subduing Māra.

The eighteen occur regularly, being interspersed with the two or three other main themes that are illustrated (Nos. 3, 5, 9, 13, 15, 17, 19, 21, 23, 25, 28, 30, 32, 34, 36, 38, 42, and 44).[9] These had all been brought to their present home from monasteries in various parts of Burma and Siam, mentioned by the writer in his description of them: Pagan, Rangoon, Mandalay, Bangkok, Lamphun, Utaradit, Dhonburi and many other places, and thus they do not reflect any special local tradition.

Other descriptions of the monasteries confirm the importance that is given to the theme of the Buddha's conquest of Māra. In an account of the Buddha images of Northern Siam, A. B. Griswold notes that 'the episode most commonly represented is his "Victory over Māra" '.[10] R. Lingat, describing the *Wat Mahādhātu,* mentions particularly the statue in the enclosure within the *Bōt*; this is 'a big statue of the Buddha in the attitude known as that of the victory over Māra (*Māravijaya*) . . . This statue is surrounded by statues of eight disciples kneeling with joined hands'.[11] Sometimes the theme is represented in painting, as in the *Wat Saket,* where the great statue of the Buddha in meditation is faced by two mural paintings, of which one is a picture of the defeat of the armies of Māra.[12]

Enough has been quoted to suggest that the conquest of Māra may justly be described as an important theme of the monastery, and monastic life. This is a direct reflection of the words of the Itivuttaka, where the life of the bhikkhu, until full enlightenment is attained, is described as a continuous battle with Māra.[13]

On the evidence of the Suttas alone it would be difficult to establish that the Māra mythology had any currency among the populace generally. Ordinary villagers could be possessed by Māra, and were, and specific examples of this are to be found,[14] but the fact was not perceived by the people themselves. A slight possibility that the idea of Māra had some popular currency may be seen in the words of Rādha: 'They say, Māra! Māra!'[15] but it is equally possible that the words 'they say' is a reference to a usage within the Buddhist fraternity. Such a finely balanced *possibility* of popular usage has to be set against the frequently emphasized idea that only the Buddha sees Māra and recognizes him, and after him, those others who like the Buddha have become awakened, those who are devoted to the Dhamma and walk in the Buddha's holy path. Further, since the Māra symbol is a doctrinal device which gathers up many points of early Buddhist teaching, as it was demonstrated in the previous chapter, it would have served as a convenient shorthand device for reminding oneself of these truths in the course of daily life, and it is evident that its value would be greatest for those whose lives were devoted to the realization and practice of these truths.

At this point account must be taken of a somewhat dissimilar view of the matter suggested by Father J. Masson, S.J.[16] This writer senses two parallel developments of the Māra symbol in the Pāli Canon, both of them stemming from a common Brahmanical original: the popular Māra, and the monastic Māra. His principal objective criterion for this division appears to be that Buddhaghosa speaks of Māra in two senses: *maccu* and *kilesa*. This he makes the basis for a division of the material on the assumption that Maccu is the popular Māra and kilesa refers to the monastic Māra.[17] The popular Māra is then identified with the picturesque, descriptive aspects of Māra, particularly in the Māra-Saṃyutta. To compare this Māra of the picturesque material with the Māra of the abstract ideas is very striking says Masson[18] (that is, for the contrast between them). Sometimes, however, the picturesque popular Māra seems to have become mixed up with the Buddhistic Māra of the abstractions: 'les courants de pensée ne sont pas absolument séparés l'un de l'autre'.[19] In other words, the material does not lend itself to this kind of division throughout, into popular and monastic. Sometimes he finds the references to Māra difficult to place exactly: these cases he regards as belonging to the stage of transition between the two conceptions of Māra.[20]. The criteria used for making this rigid kind of distinction, hypothetical and apparently all Masson's own, do not appear to be capable of producing very satisfactory results. The material in the Canon is regarded as itself providing the criteria, by its own patently analysable nature, yet the material itself is also constantly presenting the analyst with difficulties. Thus, the Dhītaro Sutta of the Māra-Saṃyutta has to be explained as a combination of these two diverse tendencies: (1) the intellectual debate represents the idea of an attack conceived in the monastic style;[21] (2) the attack made by pleasures of the senses in alluring forms, is conceived in the popular manner. This particular example of quite arbitrary analysis is further vitiated by the fact that the sense-pleasures here regarded as a 'popular' feature have already been admitted by Masson into the category of what appertains to the *'monastic'* Māra.[22] It is therefore not surprising to find that 'ces deux faces, à vrai dire, se superposent en plusieurs textes'.[23]

The purpose of this attempt to split the Māra mythology into two originally separate components appears to be to credit the laymen with the development of the popular, picturesque Māra, and the monks with the more abstract, intellectual Māra. The attempt to divide the symbol up in this way is wholly gratuitous; there is very little in the way of objective evidence to justify it. That is to say, there is no valid reason why monks should be thought to have no interest in the picturesque elements of the Māra legend, and why this should be regarded as solely for the diversion of the simple lay folk, 'the good folk who have little real understanding of the heart of the matter'[24] ('bonnes gens aux conceptions peu quintessenciées'). Indeed, to regard the Māra mythology as containing a dichotomy of this sort is precisely to miss its essential function in Theravāda Buddhism, namely that of a symbol which *connects*; a bridge between popular demonology on the one hand, and the abstract terms of the Dhamma on the other. In fact, Masson's difficulty in establishing a clear line of demarcation between what he calls the Māra of popular belief and the Māra of the abstractions provides useful confirmation of this very point, that Māra is a 'connecting' symbol. Into this symbol there run, at one extreme, strands of gross, popular demonology, and out of the symbol at the other extreme there issue abstractions pointing in the direction of the Abhidhamma. Masson's conclusion, however, is simply that the Māra mythology must be judged as 'l'un des plus anciens triomphes de la religion populaire dans le Canon pāli. . . . ' But this judgment is based upon an open and debatable point: whether what was popular, picturesque and imaginitive necessarily was without appeal to the bhikkhus. Because *some* bhikkhus and theras were learned and intellectual men, this does not mean that *all*, or even the majority were, especially in the early days of Buddhism, before the tradition of monasteries as centres of learning had developed (as it did only later, according to S. Dutt, probably in the first century AD).[25] When it is remembered that then, as now, men entered and left the Order more freely than do the members of European religious orders, and that then, as now, the monks were drawn in large measure from the ranks of village people, it will hardly be surprising that the symbol of Māra, although intended largely for those who are seeking to become Arahats, should display some popular and picturesque features.[26] The Order being what it was, it was precisely this Māra of the diverse range of features which was, entirely and understandably, the Māra of the monasteries. It is this range of features, from the picturesque on the one hand to the abstract on the other, which constitutes Māra's value as a symbol. That such a symbol should gain some currency outside the Order, among the lay people also, is by no means unlikely, but this possibility does not affect the point at issue, which is that the conception of Māra which the Canon contains is most likely to have been first developed and then faithfully preserved, not on the fringes of the Buddhist movement, but at the centre.

The indigenous animism of the Theravāda countries

The reason why it was this kind of symbol, rather than any other, by means of which the hostility and dangers which beset the holy life were depicted is not difficult to see. Māra is a symbol whose roots are in popular demonology. That is to say, the materials from which the symbol is constructed are primarily demonological materials. Such a symbol would have a particular appropriateness for the purpose of leading towards the ultimate truth those whose native mental world was largely coloured by demonological ideas. This, it has been seen, was true not only of the people of ancient India, but also of the people who inhabited those lands of South Asia in which Theravāda Buddhism established itself most strongly—Ceylon, Burma and Thailand. The main features of the popular demonology found in these lands have already been described.[27] It will readily be seen that the monk who was one of the people among whom these beliefs prevailed would find special appropriateness and value in a symbol which, on the one hand, was constructed from the kind of popular conceptions which were familiar to him, and yet which, on the other hand, served as a focus for essential Buddhist insights into the human condition, and the essential Buddhist method of dealing with it.

The radical dissimilarity between the kind of attitude to life which underlies naturalistic religion, and that which is found at the heart of Buddhism has already been noted. It is therefore obvious that for a man who had been nurtured in animistic ways of thought to become a Buddhist monk would mean a real drastic reversal of his fundamental attitudes to life. This would not be achieved all at once, and there might well be a tendency to relapse into the older habits of thought. It is at this point that the Māra symbol would prove its value. The man who had been accustomed to thinking and reacting in animistic terms, upon being subjected to some experience of ill would respond, in effect, 'How terrible! this is a yakkha. I must take such and such action (be careful, or lie low, or strike a bargain, or recite a spell, etc.)' The gap between this kind of reaction and saying, in the same distressing circumstances, 'This is Māra trying to frighten me (or disturb me etc.)! I will denounce him,' would be relatively slight compared with the gap between saying 'This is a yakkha!' and saying 'This is avijjā; I must cultivate sammā-diṭṭhi!' The latter would be a relatively large change of response to have to learn to make, at least immediately. This is perhaps a crude way of expressing how the symbol of Māra was used among the early Buddhists; how this symbol, with all its undertones of demonology and overtones of Buddhist teaching might have been found religiously helpful; but from the kind of references that have been noted in the Canon it is evident that it was in some such way as this the symbol was in fact used as an adjunct to the holy life. In support of this contention it is only necessary to compare the typical reaction of a householder to some terrifying experience that befell her in the darkness; 'How terrible for me! There is a pisāca after me!'[28] with the typical reaction of the Buddhist bhikkhunī in face of the same kind of experience: 'Now who is this . . . ? It is that foolish Māra . . . !'[29]

Moreover, in course of time, by means of its strong association (the Buddha's conquest of Māra, etc. . .) and under other Buddhist influences, the characteristically Buddhist response to experiences of evil and suffering would be so strengthened that eventually the symbol might become less and less necessary, and the disciple capable of responding without recourse to the idea of Māra; at an intermediate stage his understanding of what Māra implied and symbolized would be deepened, and his attitude to otherwise forbidding experiences become more confident. The matter may be summed up by saying that the

Pāli Buddhism of the Canon does not close the frontier of thought where it touches animism and popular demonology; it allows it to remain open, but controls it from the Buddhist side, and for Buddhist purposes. The means by which such control of this frontier between popular demonology and Buddhist doctrine and methods is maintained is the symbol of Māra, the Evil One.

NOTES

1. T. R. V. Murti, *The Central Philosophy of Buddhism*, p. 246.
2. Th. B. B. p. 68.
3. *ibid.*, p. 103.
4. *ibid.*, p. 139.
5. art., 'Popular Buddhism,' *Indian Hist. Qtly.*, 1945, p. 261.
6. Preface to PTS edition of *Thera-Therīgāthā* (1930), p. xi.
7. *The Attitudes of the Buddha*, by O. Frankfurter, JSS. Vol. X Pt. II (Bangkok), p. 2.
8. *Wat Benchamabopit and its collection of images of the Buddha*, JSS. XXII Pt I. (1928), p. 23.
9. *ibid.*, p. 24
10. *The Buddha Images of Northern Siam*, JSS. XLI Pt. 2 (January 1954), p. 109.
11. *History of the Wat Mahādhātu*, JSS. XXIV (1931), p. 8.
12. *History of the Wat Saket*, JSS XXIII (1930), p. 130.
13. It. 75.
14. e.g. *Mārasaṃyutta* II. 8 (see Appendix, pp. 119 & 121); and J III 494.
15. S III 188.
16. *La Religion Populaire dans le Canon Bouddhique Pāli* (Louvain 1942).
17. *op. cit.*, p. 100
18. *ibid.*, p. 104.
19. *ibid.*, p. 109.
20. *ibid.*, p. 104.
21. *ibid.*, p. 112.
22. *ibid.*, p. 110.
23. *ibid.*, p. 113.
24. *ibid.*, p. 103.
25. art., 'Buddhist Education', in *2500 Years of Buddhism* (Govt. of India 1956), p. 181.
26. See E. Lamotte, *HBI*, p. 687: 'Sous l'habit jaune, le moine demeure l'homme de son siècle et de son milieu.'
27. see *supra*, pp. 20 f.
28. Vin. II. 115.
29. *Bhikkhunī-Saṃyutta*, passim.

5

BEYOND MYTHOLOGY: RELIGION AND THE DEMONIC

It is a curious fact that while there is no real parallel to the Buddhist figure of Māra to be found elsewhere in Indian religion, there is a striking parallel in the New Testament, in the figure of Satan. The existence of these two similar figures provides an exercise in that kind of comparison of prominent conceptions within the major religious systems which Professor Zaehner has suggested needs to be more widely undertaken.[1] The similarities between the two will serve to reveal a common element of religious experience in Christianity and Buddhism, and in their contrasting features the symbols may possibly be seen as illuminating each other.

For the purposes of comparison with Māra, the main characteristics of Satan as he appears in the New Testament, which the writer has dealt with more fully elsewhere,[2] may be briefly recounted. It must, however, be emphasized, that it is with the Satan of the New Testament that we are concerned, and not the Satan of medieval and post-medieval Christian art.

The New Testament Symbol of Satan

(i) Satan is a mythological development emerging from a background of profuse popular demonology. This demonology is of a kind commonly found among Semitic peoples; like those of ancient India it represented a rudimentary attempt to explain and deal with the hostile, horrific and mysterious experiences of life. Like the demonology of ancient India it is of a quasi-secular rather than a religious character, in the sense that it implies a fundamentally different attitude to the ills of life from that proclaimed by the Yahwistic prophets; it looked outward, to the environment, whereas the prophets bade men look inward, into the human heart for the source of man's troubles. The virtual exclusion of demonology from the Old Testament (except for the few examples that have slipped past the prophetic censorship) is a further testimony to the fact that it was apparently regarded as belonging to secular ways of thought, rather than religious, in the Yahwistic sense. No doubt this objection was, in its explicit form, made on the grounds that these ideas were associated with false gods, or 'no-gods'. Whatever form the rejection of the popular demonology took, the basic reason was that the demonology was held to have no genuine relationship to the central truth of the religion. These notions were regarded by the prophets as non-Yahwistic, secular, false; they led men to deal with the experience of Ill in wholly *externalized* ways, and therefore, according to the prophetic view, erroneous ways. For the prophets bade men look within, and to see within the heart of man the root of evil. If primitive demonology may be regarded as providing the *thesis* in a dialetical process, prophetic religion was the *antithesis*. Nevertheless, the popular demonology appears to have persisted beneath the surface, and in the apocalyptic literature, under the influence exerted on Jewish thought by Persia, such conceptions re-asserted themselves, and were in fact admitted to the realm of religious discourse. But at the same time, these notions were, in the apocalyptic literature, moulded and developed towards the conception of a single hierarchy; it was to the unitary nature of the evil spirit-forces that the apocalyptists pointed, and to the fact that this whole force of spiritual evil was ultimately subject to the sovereignty of God. Here may be seen the dialetical *synthesis*. This is the important background of development behind the Satan of the New Testament, and it bears some striking resemblances to the way the figure of Māra developed, under the influence of a radical religion, but against the background of a primitive demonology.

(ii) Satan has the further characteristic that he is associated particularly with the evil pressures which are exerted upon the individual by man's *communal* life. Satan expresses the unholy particularly in its institutional and social manifestations, in whatever form these are manifested: in religious institutions, such as Judaism; or in political institutions, such as the Roman Empire; or in cultural forces, such as the various customs and ordinances of the pagan world. In all these areas of life Satan's activity is threefold: he is the tempter, the deceiver, and the destroyer.

(iii) There is also in the New Testament an important subsidiary feature of the demonology; this too is a mythological conception having an independent history and development, namely the principalities and powers. These tend to be subsumed in the figure of Satan, although in the New Testament they never fully are subsumed.

(iv) The Satan of the New Testament is not properly understood as a potentate in his own right. His personality has been inflated to its present formidable dimensions by the combined sins of countless individual members of human society. 'When once the spiritual principle of evil had established itself through the adoption of themselves as centres of their systems of value by all, or by any, selves, its calamitous authority would spread apace. Each would infect, and be infected, by the others. The great system of mutual support in evil would be established, which Dr Inge describes as 'co-operative guilt with limited liability'.[3]

It is this 'great system of mutual support in evil' to which the symbol of Satan in the New Testament points. Satan's power is derived collectively from the individual sins of mankind. Although he may appear monstrously imposing, and sometimes even terrible in his power, yet he has no eternal status; he is not co-eternal with God; according to the New Testament, he will have an end.

Satan and Māra: similarities and contrasts

Thus, between the symbol of Māra in the Pāli Canon and the symbol of Satan in the New Testament there are certain outstanding resemblances; they may be listed as follows.

(i) In both cases the symbols represent a thorough-going religious treatment of naturalistic or quasi-secular demon-beliefs, in which pluralism is replaced by monism, although neither in the case of Satan nor of Māra is this monism completely established; in the case of Satan the angelic powers still hover in the background, and in the case of Māra there is his somewhat vaguely conceived army or assembly, and, in addition to this, the *asura-kāya*, the relation between this anonymous evil host and the Evil One scarcely ever being considered; in the Aṇguttara-Nikāya there is a reference to Māra as 'lord of powers'[4] which might conceivably establish some relationship between Māra and the asuras, that is, one of dominance on the part of Māra. It will be noted that in both cases the symbol of the Evil One is of a kind unparalleled in the tradition to which it belongs—i.e. Hebrew or Indian.

(ii) In both cases the symbol serves as a focus for certain important doctrinal ideas; it is a doctrinal device constructed from popular demonological materials, and touches upon a number of the essential insights of the faith to which it appertains. In each case, however, it is the radical religious faith which is seen to be controlling the situation, through the symbol, rather than popular belief triumphing over the purer doctrines of the new faith. If Masson holds that the figure of Māra represents the triumph of ancient popular religious beliefs in Buddhism,[5] he must consider also the possibility that the New Testament Satan represents likewise a triumph of ancient popular belief over authentically Christian ideas. But this is not so in either case; both symbols are clearly subservient to the doctrines with which they are associated.

(iii) Both Māra and Satan symbolize the opposition which the disciple must reckon to encounter in the course of the holy life; in both cases the antagonist is regarded as having met his conqueror, in the case of Māra, the Buddha, and in the case of Satan, Christ.

(iv) Finally, in both cases the symbol may be seen to reflect a basically similar analysis of the moral evil inherent in human nature. This, however, is an item of resemblance between them which is not so apparent, and requires some elucidation. Both Māra and Satan depend, for their significance and their value as symbols, upon a prior truth about man's condition.

In the case of Satan it has been noted that he is dependent for his power upon the sins of countless individuals, the attitude of self-assertion of a host of finite, self-conscious beings. According to the New Testament view, the root cause of the evil in human existence, though it may be aggravated and magnified through the medium of man's collective life, is ultimately the assertion of the self on the part of each individual member of the race, who, because of his finitude, is unable to see the far-reaching evil effects of this self-assertion. The opposite of such self-assertion is, in the Christian view, the quality called *agape*, the quality of life manifested in Christ, and variously translated as *caritas*, charity or love.

In the Theravāda analysis the basic fault is the proneness

of men to think in terms of 'I' and 'not-I'. This is due to the roots of evil, *lobha*, *dosa* and *moha*. Moha corresponds in a sense to the inability, in the Christian analysis, of the finite individual to comprehend the entail of evil and suffering which attends self-assertion. The other two evil roots, *lobha* and *dosa*, represent the self-assertive attitudes, greed and hatred, of the morally myopic individual. Their opposites, *a-lobha* and *a-dosa*, are not in fact the negatives which their verbal form suggests, but are frequently described in terms which show their close resemblance to the quality of *agape*. The word which stands for the positive aspect of *a-lobha* and *a-dosa* is *mettā*. Eliot points out that 'the passages extolling *mettā* are numerous and striking', and adds that the *agape* of the New Testament is nearly the exact equivalent of *mettā*.[6] The striking parallel between Buddhist metta and Christian agape has also been pointed out recently by Prof Masutani.[7].

Thus both the symbol of Satan and the symbol of Māra presuppose certain basic roots of human evil. Both symbols require, for their religious understanding and use, a fairly full acquaintance with the main doctrinal ideas of the system to which each respectively belongs, and in both cases the first of these ideas, knowledge of which is assumed, is to be found in a similar view of man's defective condition. This alone does not fully account for the resemblances which exist between Satan and Māra; but it is of some significance that in their basic view of man's disorder Buddhism and Christianity are closer than is sometimes assumed.

As for the contrasts between the symbols of Satan and Māra, among a number of minor dissimilarities, two features stand out as worthy of note.

(i) In general it may be said that Māra is sometimes made to appear in a much more gross and realistic fashion than ever is the case with the Satan of the New Testament. But the the symbol of Māra itself, within the Canon, fluctuates between these grosser and other more subtle representations. The fact that, at one extreme, Māra does appear much closer to a demon than Satan is made to appear, may simply reflect the religious situation in which Māra developed, which was in some respects nearer to animism than that in which Satan developed, a few centuries later, in Judaism.

(ii) A more important distinction which has to be made

between the two symbols is with regard to the nature of the reality which they symbolize. In the case of Satan, as it has been mentioned, it is the corrupting and destructive pressure which is exerted upon the individual by the evil inherent in *man's corporate life* which is symbolized. It seemed at first to the writer that this was also the predominant theme in Māra's nature, but in the light of full investigation this view had to be rejected. In the Pāli Canon Māra is a symbol not only of 'the world' in the New Testament Johannine sense—that is, the world of men—but more than that, he symbolizes all that makes an impact upon the individual from without, all 'compounded things', human and non-human: the whole *saṃsāra* as it is known to Buddhism. It is this which constitutes the opposition to the pursuit of the holy life, rather than societary forces, as in the case of Satan. This will obviously have a bearing on the kind of response that is called for, in resisting the Evil One, in Buddhist and in Christian thought and practice respectively.

It is obvious, however, that when differences have been allowed for, there remain some impressive parallels between these two symbols. These have been noted, in greater or lesser degree, by a number of writers in the past, and various explanations have been offered. Some were inclined to think there had been borrowing, either of Buddhist ideas by Christians, or vice versa. The similarity has often been remarked between the stories of the temptation of the Buddha and of Christ. Ernst Windisch dealt fairly fully with the various views which had been put forward concerning the relationship of these two narratives. He came to the conclusion that the differences in the two narratives are as striking as the similarities.[8] Moreover, although the Māra legend is historically the earlier of the two, there are no grounds for assuming any knowledge of this legend in Palestine; such knowledge is, Windisch adds, highly improbable. The difficulty with which the legend would be transmitted is fairly obvious, in view of the piecemeal nature of the Māra mythology, scattered as it is throughout the texts. The important dissimilarities in the sequence of events in the case of Christ's temptation, compared with the Buddha's, have been examined and are set out at length by E. J. Thomas in his *Life of Buddha*.[9]

Literary dependence of one narrative, or collection of narratives, upon the other seems, therefore, fairly clearly ruled out. Subsequent studies appear in no way to have shaken Windisch's general conclusion on the matter: 'The two may be taken only as parallel appearances. Taken as such they are of great importance for the history of comparative religion, and for the history of the forms which religious thought assumes'. In each case, he considers, the symbol of the Evil One grew out of the distinctive doctrine—Māra out of the doctrine of the Buddha, and Satan out of Christ's gospel of redemption.[10] In each case the symbol came into being as the result of the experience and insight of a great personality. In each case it appears to have reflected the experience of critical encounter with a spiritual force which was hostile to holiness.

It has been suggested in the course of this study that the demons of popular thought are to be understood in terms of men's experiences of the uncanny, the dreadful, the menacing aspects of life. It has also been suggested that in radical contrast to this attitude were the Buddhist and Christian views which saw behind the same kind of phenomena a quite different significance; between the animistic attitude to the uncanny and the eerie, and the Buddhist attitude towards it the difference is not one of degree merely, but of kind. This conclusion must obviously be justified more fully in view of the well-known theories put forward by Rudolf Otto in his *Idea of the Holy*.

In that work he claimed that what he called 'daemonic dread' is an antecedent stage of what at higher levels may be termed religious awe. This daemonic dread, he claims, 'first begins to stir in the feeling of "something uncanny", "eerie" or "weird". It is this feeling which, emerging in the mind of primeval man, forms the starting point for the entire religious development in history. "Daemons" and "gods" alike spring from this root, and all the products of "mythological apperception" or "fantasy" are nothing but different modes in which it has been objectified. And all ostensible explanations of the origin of religion in terms of animism or magic or folk psychology are doomed from the outset to wander astray and miss the real goal of their inquiry, unless they recognize this fact of our nature—primary, unique, underivable from anything else—to be the basic factor and the basic impulse underlying the entire process of religious evolution.'[11]

The view of the demonic which has been taken in the course of this study is clearly not in accord with Otto's dictum that this sense of the uncanny is the basic impulse underlying the entire process of religious evolution. Otto's view was criticized by B. H. Streeter in his Bampton Lectures.[12] It is not necessary to do more than refer briefly to what Streeter wrote there. He noted that the inaugural vision of Isaiah, which Otto would claim as an illustration of the numinous, was very different 'not in degree but in kind, from anything to which by any stretch of language could be applied adjectives like "uncanny" "eerie" or "daemonic".' He pointed out that Otto was not blind to this difference of quality, and was indeed trying to account for it when he spoke of 'the moralizing and rationalizing process' that the numinous has undergone in the religion of the prophets and of Christ.[13] He noted further that Otto was reduced to desperate straits when he tried to make his theory fit the teaching of the New Testament, and especially that of Christ.[14] The poverty of Otto's argument with regard to the New Testament was demonstrated in detail by Streeter. It is particularly clear in the light of Pauline and Johannine teaching, and Streeter carries conviction when he says that it would seem to follow, from St Paul's doctrine of justification, and the Johannine antithesis of love and fear, that 'the more completely a man becomes a Christian, the less there will be of the numinous in his experience of God—a remarkable phenomenon if the numinous is in any sense the *basis* of religion.'[15]

The same has been observed to be true of Pāli Buddhism. *Bhaya*—fear—fear of the dark aspect of life, or of the uncanny, is of Māra; again and again this has been noticed. The light of the Buddha disperses the darkness of Māra like the sunshine dispersing the gloomy clouds. There could be no clearer contrast. The claims of popular demonology to be taken seriously as an early form of the same quality of feeling which in later stages emerges as Buddhist enlightenment could not be more seriously discountenanced than they are in the unequivocally antagonistic relations which exist between Māra and the Buddha. It is in the total elimination of Māra and all the (numinous) sensations which he elicits that the experience of enlightenment partly consists. Far from the experience of 'shudder' being an essential element of higher religion, as Otto claims (although in a form 'ennobled beyond measure'), in so far as it is present at all in the human consciousness it is regarded in Buddhist thought as a direct indication that a man has *not yet* entered into the higher experience of his religion. The most that can be said in favour of Otto's theory is that the 'numinous' requires careful restatement, in terms rather of 'holy awe' than merely demonic dread, and its developments.

With regard to Pāli Buddhism, the conclusion must stand which Streeter drew with regard to the Christian teaching of the New Testament. Between the expression of man's experience of Ill, the uncanny, the dark and the menacing, in terms of demonic beings, and the *summum bonum* of Buddhism, i.e. nirvāna, there is radical cleavage rather than continuity. This has been pointed out by R. N. Smart, who writes: 'Given Otto's analysis of his own illuminating expression "numinous", nirvāna is not, strictly speaking, numinous; but nirvāna is the key concept of (at least Lesser Vehicle) Buddhist doctrine and practice; hence it is unsatisfactory to define religion by reference to the numinous and analogous notions.'[16]

Numinous fear must therefore be regarded as an experience characteristic of animism and other forms of naturalistic religion, but not of radical systems of belief which are based on inward illumination. H. H. Farmer makes a similar distinction: 'There is nothing essentially religious in the belief in the *demons, devils or evil spirits* of various kinds with which men, on both primitive and higher levels have so frequently peopled their world.'[17] In the case of the religions of Buddhism and Christianity there is a different interpretation of the uncanny and evil elements of existence, a different emotion is elicited, and a different response is called for; the parallel between the two kinds of attitude may be set out as follows:

	1 *Popular, or naturalistic*	2 *Radical, or A-naturalistic*
The datum:	evils of life	evils of life
Interpretation of it:	demons	Evil One
Emotion elicited:	numinous fear	indifference or confident resistance?
Response indicated:	repelling or evasive action, of an *external* kind.	steadfastness of *inward* faith and contemplation of the Holy.

In so far as numinous fear is present at all in 'higher' religion, (and if when present it is really homogeneous with demonic dread and horror) this 'fear' may equally well be explained as due to uneradicated traces of popular, animistic feelings. It would be unrealistic to assume that such traces could not be found. What Otto says regarding the persistence of the numinous at every level of religion may be regarded as demonstrating that naturalistic feelings in religious matters do not yield easily, and that the supreme experiences to which Buddhism or Christianity call men are, as long as mortal life lasts, fraught with danger, and must be pursued diligently, albeit confidently, in the face of the Ill of life, towards which too easily a wrong attitude can re-develop. The Devil, who in a single being embodies the diverse devils of popular thought, is the constant enemy of the life of renunciation and self-denial. 'Watch and pray, lest you enter into temptation,' Christ exhorts his disciples.[18] 'Meditate, bhikkhus, and do not be slothful, lest afterwards you experience remorse,' is the almost identical exhortation of the Buddha.[19] At first the disciple may learn to watch, to meditate, with the idea that he must be strong against the Evil One, and this mythological conception may be a great aid to his perseverance and steadfastness: the thought-forms in which he was nurtured are used to guide him along the road which he needs to follow. But Satan and Māra are *symbols*; this means that their function is principally to facilitate a transition of viewpoint for those accustomed to thinking in demonic terms, rather than to embody absolute truth. The mythological figures are means to an end, rather than ends in themselves. Much distortion of Christian thinking where Satan is concerned might have been avoided if his symbolic nature had been accepted, in the sense which is inescapable in any careful study of the New Testament. The mythological and incidental features which are inevitable in such a portrait would not then have been fastened upon as accurate delineations of a real creature. To regard Satan in the latter way is to have slipped back into primitive demonology, rather than to have been pointed forward by the symbol to a realization of the universal, cosmic hostility which man encounters in his strivings after that which has been revealed to him. All this is equally true of Māra.

The conquest of the demonic, and the two aspects of religion

Before some final conclusions are suggested as a result of this comparison of Māra and Satan it is necessary to consider the possible question: in what sense do these two symbols stand for the same reality? May not the resemblances be superficial only, in view of the *fundamental* difference between Buddhism and Christianity (on which a great deal of emphasis is sometimes laid), namely the difference between a system which is described as atheistic, and one which is in the general sense theistic?

The reply which is suggested here is that it is possible to see in the similarity of these two symbols evidence of a common area of religious experience, which shows the two systems to be closer together than their differences would suggest. In other words, before Buddhism and Christianity are judged to be opposed in their fundamentals, let careful consideration be given to this element of experience which is common to both. Perhaps, after all, it will be found that what they have in common is at least as impressive as what divides them.

It is now clear that both Māra and Satan represent a force which proves resistant to man's search for holiness. This opposing force is conceived as being so potent and so hard to overcome by man, so universally active and so malign, that it is endowed with a will and personality. 'The demonic', in the sense in which it is often referred to by Paul Tillich, satisfactorily comprehends what is meant here, and makes a useful shorthand term.

In the case of Māra the demonic is conceived primarily in terms of the deluding effect upon the individual of the whole saṃsāra, which exerts an ensnaring, entangling influence upon him, and against which his defence is the practice of ardent meditation and the cultivation of insight. The demonic is not regarded as consisting in any special way of *social* forces, and no special attention appears to be given to the social dimension of religious life; there is no particular concern in this case with reinforcing the life of the individual at this level. But because this aspect of the matter does not receive explicit recognition in the symbol of Māra, this is not to say that Buddhism as a religious system is oblivious to the need for a social dimension; implicitly this is acknowledged in the way the Saṇgha has developed; it is with the regulating of the life of this community that the first section of the Canon, the Vinaya Piṭaka, is concerned.[20]

In the case of Satan the demonic is symbolized as predominantly social and cultural. It is to be resisted by the experience of participation in a new kind of societary life. Satan is dispelled and defeated by the Holy Spirit, and this emphasis within the Christian tradition is reflected in the fact that to be a Christian is a matter of being a member of a community, a new society which is (in theory at least) distinguished from all other forms of society by the kind of relationships which exist among its members. The theory of the matter is that the Christian's security againt the spiritual adversary is a *common* security, it is one which he enjoys in so far as he experiences the corporate life of the Christian society, the koinōnia, the fellowship of the Holy Spirit.

But what the references to Satan in the New Testament do not indicate at all clearly (unlike the Buddist references to the Evil One) is the urgent necessity for prayer and contemplation. Soberness and vigilance are called for, and the saint should be mindful of Satan's wiles; in writing to the Ephesians the apostle reminds them of their spiritual adversary, and urges them to pray at all times in the Spirit, with all prayer and supplication. But in general it cannot be said that the mention of the name of Satan constitutes an automatic reminder of the prime importance of private meditation, in the way that the mention of Māra does in the Buddhist texts. Nevertheless, in Christian practice the imperative need for this arm of spiritual warfare has constantly been acknowledged. It may be said that in general, wherever this has been neglected, Christian vitality has been impaired, and where it has been taken seriously a wide circle has often benefited as a result. It is thus obvious that the Christian tradition demonstrates that one of the most potent weapons with which the adversary can be overcome is prayer and meditation, as Buddhism insists. Here, then, is where the symbol of Satan, as it may be understood from the teaching given about him in the New Testament, gives only a partial account of the real situation.

Thus in the case of the Buddhist symbol of Māra, and that of the New Testament symbol of Satan, it is true to say that each symbol only partially symbolizes the reality which, as other indications show, both traditions are aware of as an opposition which has to be met not only individually but socially also; not only corporately but also privately.

The reason for the special emphasis which each of the symbols reveals is not hard to find. The figures of Satan and of Māra were not constructed artificially, with the advantage of the hindsight of the centuries which is now being applied to them. Each is a symbolization which expresses the special emphasis of a particular religious and historical situation. The symbols grew spontaneously, each in its own environment; Māra in the climate of Indian religious philosophy and psychology, with its overriding emphasis upon the idea of the existence through countless rebirths of the individual; Satan in the climate of Judaism, with its keen awareness of corporate realities—the seed of Abraham, the people of Israel, the kingdom of David, the Jewish nation: such conceptions are the essential background of the New Testament symbol of Satan. Thus the religious and historical environment in each case influenced and moulded the conception of the supernatural conflict, in which there was felt to be an evil power and a good, Māra and the eternal Dhamma, Satan and the Holy Spirit. It is not that Theravāda Buddhism and Christianity represent diametrically opposite religious emphases, the Theravāda standing exclusively for the individualistic dimension in religion, and Christianity for the social dimension. Plainly this is not so. But in the historical situation in which these symbols were formulated the demonic was conceived in these two different ways; each is the symbol which was valid in a particular historical religious situation. But this fact, that each of them separately symbolizes only one aspect of an opposition which is twofold, and which both traditions implicitly acknowledge to be twofold, indicates that the symbols are in some sense complementary. Here is to be seen an example of how two major religious traditions may learn from each other; the symbols may illuminate each other: for what they symbolize is better understood in the light of both symbols than in the light of either one of them alone.

The importance of a modern restatement of the demonic

Buddhism, unlike Christianity, is not a dogmatic religion; that is to say, it does not proclaim a *kerygma* as the basis of faith, but rather it bids men come and experience for themselves (*Ehi passiko*). It is not a credal system in the sense that Christianity is, with its affirmations of certain historical and theological events and their significance. In view of this, the fact that Buddhism knows a Devil has some striking implications. That such a figure, so graphically portrayed, can be found in a non-dogmatic, non-credal system is another indication that the Evil One is only a symbol, an aid; its importance is relative, not absolute. The point may be put in another way by saying that the figure of Māra represents an *approach* to the Dhamma (from animism), but is no part of the Dhamma itself. Whether the symbol of Māra is of much or little religious value to a man will depend on his initial viewpoint; whether Māra is regarded as a grossly demonological or a more subtly metaphysical symbol will depend upon the degree of understanding which he has reached. Māra is to be regarded in whatever way it is most useful to regard him; he is a doctrinal device, not an item of doctrine.

It is instructive to consider that the same may equally be true of Satan. Sometimes in Christian thought Satan is considered solely from the point of view of what is Christian doctrine and what is not. If Satan, as he is described in the New Testament, can be regarded as an item of orthodox doctrine, then he may be accepted; if he cannot strictly be so regarded, then he must be rejected altogether—so the argument (perhaps unconsciously) sometimes runs.

But in the light of this comparison of the Buddhist and Christian symbols, it seems likely that the more appropriate approach to the question of Satan's existence is not, 'Do you believe in Satan?'—for it depends who you are, and what is your cultural and mental background, whether you believe in Satan: that is, whether *this particular symbol* has relevance for you. But the New Testament suggests that what Satan symbolizes is real for everyone: an opposition to holiness which is something more than mere inertia and is a force with an animus of its own. This is real, in whatever terms it is described, and by whatever symbol it is represented. It is precisely because there is symbol *and* reality that the two must be distinguished, so that when the symbol is rejected for one reason or another, the reality is not disregarded.

For it is clear that the symbol of Satan (and of Māra) is likely to become weak and attenuated when the type of belief out of which it emerged is weakened under the influence of scientific thought. This is largely what has happened to the symbol of Satan in modern western life. But if the symbol has had its day, this is not to say that the reality which it symbolized has also passed away. The reality remains, and religion has to take account of it, and come to grips with it.

If, because the symbol is outworn and irrelevant in a scientific age, it is discarded, then the reality to which it pointed has no longer any representation by means of which men may be constantly reminded of it. There is thus a need to find other effective ways of speaking of this reality which these symbols formerly represented, ways that will be relevant to modern man's understanding of his existence. In the attempt to do this a full appreciation of all that Māra and Satan represented will be essential; essential also will be an appreciation of the way in which they represented it, that is by the use of conceptions borrowed from popular contemporary belief.

Such an appreciation of the significance of the symbol of Māra within the living tradition of Buddhism it has been the aim of this study to establish, as a contribution to the work of re-interpretation.

NOTES

1. *At Sundry Times* (London, 1958), p. 11 f.
2. *The Significance of Satan* (London, 1960)
3. Wm. Temple, *Nature, Man and God* (London, 1934), p. 369 f.
4. A. II. 17 (and see Appendix, p. 113).
5. see *supra*, p. 77.
6. *HB* Vol. I, p. 184.
7. F. Masutani, *A Comparative Study of Buddhism and Christianity* (Tokyo 1957), pp. 163-174.
8. *Māra und Buddha* (Leipzig, 1895), p. 214
9. *The Life of Buddha*, p. 239 f.
10. *Māra und Buddha*, p. 219.
11. *The Idea of the Holy* (London, 1923), p. 15.
12. *The Buddha and the Christ* (London, 1932).
13. Streeter, *op. cit.*, p. 317.
14. *ibid.*, p. 318.
15. *ibid.*, p. 323.
16. *Church Quarterly Review*, Apr.-June 1959, p. 216.
17. *Revelation and Religion* (London, 1954), p. 90.
18. *grēgoreite kai proseuchesthe, hina mē eiselthēte eis peiriasmon*—Matt. 26. 41.
19. *Jhāyatha, bhikkhave, mā pamādattha, mā pacchā vippaṭisārino ahuvattha*—M I. 118.
20. On the socialization of the originally eremetical Buddhist way of life, see S. Dutt, *Early Buddhist Monachism—600 B.C.–100 B.C.* (London, 1924), pp. 112–134.

APPENDIX

SURVEY OF THE REFERENCES TO MĀRA THE EVIL ONE CONTAINED IN THE PĀLI CANON

FOR the benefit of the reader who requires a more detailed exposition of the matters which have been dealt with in the foregoing pages the following survey of the references to Māra to be found in the books of the Pāli Canon is provided.

The Sutta Piṭaka is examined first, since the great majority of the references are to be found there. The method followed is to examine the constituent parts of this Piṭaka book by book. In this way the extent and the frequency of the references is more fully appreciated. After this the references contained in the Vinaya Piṭaka are surveyed. There is very little material of this kind in the third section of the Canon, the Abhidhamma-Piṭaka, and the significance of this fact was dealt with in Chapter 2 above. What few allusions do occur are briefly noted.

I DĪGHA NIKĀYA

(1) First to be considered among the references to Māra the Evil One are those which occur regularly in the Nikāyas in certain conventionally worded formulas. These consist of a form of description of the Buddha as one 'who knows the universe, with its devas, with Māra, with Brahmā; the whole creation, with recluse and brahman, the world of men and devas, by his own supernatural insight he knows.' (*So imaṃ lokaṃ sadevakaṃ, samārakaṃ sabrahmakaṃ sassamaṇabrāhmaniṃ pajaṃ sadeva-manussaṃ sayaṃ abhiññā.*—D I. 87; I. 111; I. 150; I. 224; III. 77)

This formula is sometimes taken by translators to imply a plurality of Māras. By analogy with sadevakam, it would seem natural to give samārakam this meaning, since devas are known in the plural.

Over against this, however, is the fact that apart from this ambiguous evidence, there is no other direct evidence in the Canon of a belief in a multiplicity of Māras; there are devas of the Māra group, but this is another matter.

Other examples of this kind of formula, intended apparently to comprehend all types of beings, are found elsewhere. In the Mahāpadāna Sutta, for example, it is said that at the time of the birth of a Bodhisatta a noble radiance appears throughout the world—*sadevake loke samārake sabrahmake sassamaṇa-brāhmaṇiyā pajāya* etc. (D II. 12 and 15). The Editors of the PTS Dictionary suggest as the translation here, 'the world with its devas, its Māra, its Brahmā . . . etc.'[1] A similar version of the formula occurs in the Mahāparinibbāna Suttanta (D II. 127), where it was translated by T. W. Rhys Davids as singular: 'I see no one, Chunda, on earth, or in Māra's heaven, etc.'. An interesting variant of the formula occurs in two other passages. In the Agañña Suttanta it is said that he whose faith is in the Tathāgata has a faith which cannot be destroyed 'by recluse or brahmin or deva or Māra or Brahmā' (*samaṇena vā brahmaṇena vā devena vā Mārena vā Brahmunā.* D III. 84). In the *Lakkhaṇa Suttanta* (D III. 146) the same wording is used when it is said that the Buddha is not liable to obstruction from any foe or adversary within or without . . . 'whether recluse or brahmin, etc.' The fact that these nouns occur in the instrumental *singular* is still not decisive evidence in favour of Māra existing only in the singular, for the singular form is used here of other nouns, all of which *are* known to exist in a plural sense; this could therefore be true also of the word *mārena.* From the evidence provided by these conventional formulas alone it seems impossible to determine whether Māra is to be regarded as one or many, and translators seem to favour now one, now the other alternative. A passage in the *Saṅgīti Suttanta* suggests that the answer lies somewhere between the two alternatives, for in a list of eight different kinds of assemblies of beings, there is mention of '*Māra-parisā*' (D III. 260). This appears to be a conception similar to that which will be met elsewhere, of the Māra-army (*Mārasenā*). The beings who compose this assembly or army are, however, not thought of as having any identity apart from being agents of Māra; it is the figure of Māra which predominates.

(II) *References to Māra: Legendary*

The second class of references to Māra are those which undoubtedly refer to a single figure. In the Sutta of the Great

[1] See under *Loka,* col. 1.

Concourse, among the hosts of spirit-beings who present themselves are the Asuras. The names of some of these are given: the 'Kālakañjas, the Dānaveghasas, Vepacitti, Sucitti, Pahārāda, and Namuci with them . . . . ' (followed by further names D II. 259). The occurrence here, among the Asuras, of the name Namuci is noteworthy, since this is elsewhere used as a name for Māra (e.g. *Sutta-Nipāta* 426, 429). Here, however, Namuci appears to occupy a position of no particular prominence, as Māra usually does. What is more, the name does not, in this case, appear to be a synonym for Māra, for having appeared here in the list of celestial beings who had come to pay homage, Namuci must be regarded as one of these assembled devas who all, at the end of the Suttanta, are alike Māra's intended victims: '*Te ca sabbe abbhikkante . . . Māra-senā abbhikkāmi,*' (D II. 261) These lines may therefore be regarded as evidence of a tradition which regarded Namuci as another spirit-being originally separate from Māra, a tradition having its roots in Indian mythology.

Of particular interest are the last two paragraphs of the Mahāsamaya Suttanta. The approach of Māra's army, which has just been mentioned, gives the Suttanta a dramatic and striking conclusion. Māra, the Great General (*Mahāseno*) suddenly appears and bids his 'dark hosts' (*kaṇha-senā*)[1] surround and seize and bind the whole assembly with the bond of lust, letting none escape: '*Etha gaṇhatha bandatha rāgena baddam atthu ve, samantā parivāretha mā vo muñcittha koci naṃ*' (D II. 262). In the text this command is preceded by a narrator's remark bidding the reader observe the stupidity or folly of Māra in what follows: '*Passa Kaṇhassa mandiyam . . .*' This remark is significant, and may well indicate one of the main purposes here, namely: to expose the folly of Māra.

The Āṭānāṭiya *rakkhaṃ* (D III. 195 ff.) contains an interesting reference to *Māra-senā*. The rakkhaṃ begins with an ascription of praise to seven Buddhas, each of whom is named together with an appropriate attribute. The fourth in the list, Kakusandha, is described as 'crusher of Māra's host (*Māra-senā-pamaddino* D III. 196). This and the six different attributes applied to the other six Buddhas named constitute a conventional list of the characteristic qualities of a Buddha; all

[1] or 'Kaṇha's hosts'; *Kaṇha* as an alternative name for Māra is used in this passage. (D II. 261.)

the seven, says Buddhaghosa, are equally applicable to all the Buddhas. It is therefore worthy of note that one of the essential features of a Buddha is that he is *Māra-senā-pamadinno.*

The *Mahā-Parinibbāna Sutta* contains the next passage to be considered. According to the version of this sutta found in the Dīgha, Māra had previously approached the Buddha on the bank of the Nerañjarā, immediately after the Enlightenment, and had urged the Buddha to enter directly into Parinibbāna: *Parinibbātu dāni bhante Bhagavā, parinibbātu Sugato, parinibbāna-kālo dāni bhante Bhagavato* (D II. 112). The underlying assumption in this legend seems to be that Māra was anxious that knowledge of the Enlightenment should not be spread abroad. To this the Buddha replied at some length, the gist of his reply being that he would not enter Nibbāna until this pure religion should have become successful, prosperous, widespread and popular. '*Na tāvāhaṃ pāpima parinibbāyissāmi yāva me idaṃ brahmacariyaṃ na iddhañ c'eva bhavissati phītañ ca vitthārikaṃ bāhujaññaṃ puthu-bhūtaṃ, yāvad eva manussehi suppakāsitan-ti*'. In other words, the Buddha anticipates precisely what Māra had hoped to prevent. The Mahā-parinibbāna sutta takes up the narrative at the point where this purpose of the Buddha had now been accomplished. The Buddha relates to Ānanda that Māra has now approached him again, and again urged him to pass into Parinibbāna, on exactly the grounds that the Buddha's original purpose had now been fulfilled. This time the Buddha appears to agree with the suggestion made by Māra—an agreement between these two which is without parallel. The Buddha replies: '*Appossukko tvaṃ pāpima hohi, na ciraṃ Tathāgataparinibbānaṃ bhavissati, ito tiṇṇaṃ māsānaṃ accayena Tathāgato parinibbāyissati* (D II. 106). What is clear to the reader is that the Buddha is entirely uninfluenced by Māra's suggestions, even when apparently he chooses a course of action which coincides with that suggested by Māra; in his encounters with the Buddha Māra effects nothing. It will be noted, however, that Māra *is* regarded as being able to 'possess' the mind of Ānanda (D II. 103).

(III) *References to Māra: Didactic*

So far the material concerning Māra, apart from the conventional formulas, has been of what may be called a legendary nature; that is, it has consisted of stories about Māra. There is another type of Māra-material, besides the legendary, which may be called 'didactic'. This classification will, as far as possible, be followed throughout the examination of the Māra-material in the Canon, but it should not be allowed to obscure the fact that a great deal of what is legendary in form is *also* didactic in purpose.

In the Dīgha Nikāya such didactic material is found in the *Cakkavatti-sīhanāda Suttanta*. The Exalted One is addressing the bhikkhus: 'Keep to your own pastures, brethren, walk in your native haunts. If you thus walk in them the Evil One will find no landing place, no basis of attack.' (D III. 58). At the end of the Suttanta, after the story of King Strongtyre and his sons, these words are repeated, with a variation: 'Keep to your own pastures, brethren, walk in your native haunts. If you so walk you shall grow in length of years . . . in comeliness . . . in happiness . . . in wealth . . . in power.' These five ways of growth take the place here of the words '*the Evil One will find no landing place, no basis of attack*.' Each of the five then receives detailed explanation; they are associated with (1) the Four Iddhipādas; (2) right conduct (3) entry into and abiding in the Four Jhānas (4) love-burdened thought and (5) destruction of the deadly taints. At the end of this exposition the Buddha adds: 'I consider no power, brethren, so hard to subdue as the power of Māra. But this merit expands, brethren, by the taking up into oneself of that which is good' (D III 77).

2 MAJJHIMA NIKĀYA

The references to Māra, in the Majjhima as in the Dīgha, may be divided into three groups: (i) conventional cosmic formulas; (ii) legendary material, that is, stories of human encounters with Māra; (iii) didactic material, that is, teaching about Māra given by the Buddha.

(1) There are some sixteen examples in the Majjhima Nikāya of the mention of Māra in cosmic formulas and descriptions. Eleven of these are in lists of beings which are intended to convey comprehensive or exhaustive descriptions of the human and the deva- world. These correspond very closely with those already examined in the Dīgha Nikāya; examples are as follows: *Tatra vata maṁ samaṇo vā brāhmaṇo vā devo vā Māro*

vā Brahmā vā koci lokasmiṁ (M. I. 71, 72). An example of a similar kind occurs at I. 384. '*Nāhan taṁ passāmi sadevake loke samārake sabrahmake sassamaṇabrāhmaniyā pajāya sadevamanussāya ....*' (M I. 85 and 143; III. 60, 77, 120, 123, 248, 252). Three further instances of the same kind of formula are distinguished by the fact that this whole cosmic hierarchy is said to be seen by the Buddha, or Tathāgata, 'by his own supernatural knowledge', and made known: (*so imaṁ lokaṁ sadevakaṁ samārakaṁ sabrahmakaṁ sassamaṇabrāhmaniṁ pajaṁ sadevamanussaṁ sayaṁ abhiññā sacchikatvā pavedeti.*' (M I, 179 and 401; II. 133.)

Mention of Māra's assembly (Māra-parisā) in a list of eight kinds of assemblies occurs again in the Majjhima, as in the Dīgha. (M I. 72). The Pāli commentary on this passage expressly says that these *Māra-parisās* are to be understood not as 'assemblies of Māras, but occasions when those in Māra's retinue gather together. The commentator clearly regards Māra himself as one, rather than many. In the Bahudhātuka Sutta (M III. 66) Māra's name occurs is a list of four supernatural beings, who, it is said, a woman could not become (although a man could). These four are, in order: a Sammāsambuddha, Sakka, Māra and Brahmā. These recurrent formulas, and the last especially, provide evidence that Māra's place in the Buddhist hierarchy is one of considerable eminence.

(II) The legendary material in this Nikāya is found in the last two Suttas of the *Mūlapaṇṇāsa*. A personal encounter of the Buddha with Māra is described in the first of these, and of Mogallāna with Māra in the second.

1. It is related in the Brahmanimantaṇika Sutta (M I. 326 f) that the Buddha had come to know that Baka the Brahmā was entertaining false views, that is, he was regarding that which was impermanent as permanent, etc.; *Idaṁ niccaṁ idaṁ dhuvaṁ idaṁ sassataṁ idaṁ kevalaṁ* etc. ('*Idaṁ*', says the Pāli commentator, refers here to a *Brahmaṭṭhana* (M A II. 405). Thereupon, vanishing from Sāvatthī, the Buddha appeared in the Brahma world. Baka the Brahmā, having repeated his erroneous affirmations, was corrected by the Buddha, who told him most emphatically that his false view was the outcome of *avijjā*: '*Avijjāgato vata bho Bako brahmā avijjāgato vata bho Bako brahmā, yatra hi nāma aniccaṁ yeva samānam niccan-ti vakkhati ...*' (M I. 326).

At this point Māra intervened. Having entered into a company of Brahmās he spoke words of warning to the Buddha (he is represented as speaking through the Brahmās): 'Bhikkhu, do not meddle with this. For this Brahmā is a Mahābrahmā, Victor, Unvanquished, All-seeing, Controller, Lord, Maker, Creator, Chief Disposer, Master, Father of all that have become and will be.' Māra further informed the Buddha that his foolish denials of the truths which Baka had affirmed were by no means the first to be made—there had been scornful samaṇas before Gotama, and these all had been reborn in woeful ways; it would therefore be better for the Buddha to accept what Baka had affirmed, and not to persist in his foolish opposition. To all of this the Buddha made the characteristic reply: '*Jānāmi kho tāhaṁ pāpima, mā tvaṁ maññittho: na maṁ jānātīti, māro tvam asi pāpima.*' (M I. 327). This power of the Buddha to recognize Māra immediately is an important feature of the legendary material, and will be encountered repeatedly. It is this which frustrates all Māra's efforts against the Buddha. Moreover, not only did the Buddha recognize and denounce Māra the Evil One; he also in this case makes clear that he was not impressed by the power of the Brahmā companies, since these all were in Māra's power, whereas he, the Buddha was not in Māra's power: '*Yo c'eva pāpima Brahmā yā Brahmaparisā ye ca Brahmapārisajjā sabbe va tava hatthagatā sabbe va tava vasagatā . . . Ahaṁ ko pana pāpima n'eva tava hatthagato* . . . .' (M I. 327).

After further conversation with Baka, in the course of which the Buddha's superior knowledge was demonstrated, the Buddha departed from the Brahma world, leaving its inhabitants marvelling at the psychic power and majesty of Gotama Sakyaputta. He was then approached once more by Māra; again, not directly, but through a conclave of Brahmās. This time the Evil One urged the Buddha to keep his supernatural knowledge to himself, and warned him in similar terms as before not to communicate it to the disciples, lest he too should be reborn in woe. Once again the Buddha replied by identifying Māra as the speaker: '*Jānāmi kho tāhaṃ pāpima*, etc.' This time the Buddha added that he was fully aware of Māra's motives in speaking thus to him; it was not, as he pretended, because he was well-disposed towards the Buddha, but rather the reverse; Māra was anxious to prevent others passing from his reach, and this he foresaw would happen if the Buddha went on teaching his *Dhamma* to disciples. The Buddha's address to Māra concluded with a declaration that he, unlike previous claimants, was indeed *sammāsaṁbuddha*, whether or not he taught and communicated *Dhamma* to his disciples; that is to say, he was certainly no less a *sammāsaṁbuddha* because he taught (M I. 330 f.).

2. The *Māratajjaniya Sutta* (M I. 332-8) records Moggallāna's encounter with Māra. Moggallāna, it is said, was pacing up and down in the open air at Suṁsumaragira when Māra got into his stomach. As this occasioned Moggallāna severe discomfort he sat down to reflect on the possible cause. Quickly he understood that it was Māra, and addressed the Evil One, making plain to him that he had been recognized: '*Nikkhama pāpima, nikkhama pāpima.*' (M I. 332) Māra then began to soliloquize, astonished that Moggallāna had recognized him so quickly. Hearing this, Moggallāna replied that he had indeed recognized him. The same form of words is attributed to Moggallāna as to the Buddha in similar circumstances, and their repetition emphasizes again the importance that was attached to an ability to recognize Māra (. . . *mā tvaṃ maññittho: na maṃ jānātī ti, Māro tvam asi pāpima*—M I. 332). Moggallāna then embarked upon a long anecdote to illustrate the folly involved in attacking a bhikkhu, and this makes up the rest of the sutta. The anecdote tells of the time when Kakusandha was Buddha, and a certain Dūsin was Māra. A curious feature of the story is that Moggallāna identifies himself with Dūsin; this was his former existence; Kāḷī was the name of his sister and her son was (the present) Māra, who is thus Moggallāna's nephew. *Bhūtapubbāhaṁ pāpima Dūsī nāma māro ahosiṁ, tassa me Kāḷī nāma bhaginī, tassā tvaṁ putto, so me tvaṁ bhāgineyyo hosi.* (M I. 333).

The story relates how this Dūsin, in order to obtain an opportunity (*otāra*) against the disciples of the Buddha Kakusandha, incited some villagers to abuse and revile them. When this failed he incited the villagers to flatter them, hoping to obtain an opportunity against them in this way, but again without success. He then took possession of a young man and caused him to throw a stone and split open the head of one of the bhikkhus, the venerable Vidhura, while he and the Lord, Kakusandha, were on their morning alms-round. At a look from the Lord, Dūsin the Māra died and arose in the great Niraya Hell, where he suffered terrible torment for many thousands of years. The point of the story is made in the verses which are appended to it, which contain the recurrent line 'O Dark one (*Kaṇha*), for striking such a monk you go to suffering.' These verses are found also in the Theragāthā (1187-1208), where they are addressed to Māra. The concluding lines emphasize the idea that Māra is capable of acquiring demerit for assailing a Tathāgata (the same idea will be found again in the Māra Saṃyuttas), although Māra himself may believe that for him evil does *not* mature (*kin-nu maññasi pāpima: na me pāpaṁ vipaccati, Karoto cīyati pāpaṁ cirarattāya Antaka*'. (M I. 338).

The sutta ends with the words '*tato so dummano yakkho tatth 'ev 'antaradhāyathāti* a formula occurring over and over again at the sutta endings in the Māra Saṁyutta. It is of interest in that it links this narrative with that traditional type of Māra-story, as Windisch observes (*Māra und Buddha*, p. 160); although, as he notes also, this narrative has general affinities with the Jātaka type of story (*ibid.*, p. 149). The reference to Māra as a yakkha is also of special interest.

It is possible to distinguish two or possibly three originally separate elements which may have been put together to give the sutta its present form. These are: (1) the exordium, consisting of the legend of Moggallāna's discomfiture by Māra and Māra's being recognized and expelled (2) the story of Dūsin the Māra; (3) the concluding verses, which are found also in the Theragāthā (1187-1208). As the verses occur there independently of the story of Dūsin, it is possible that the present form of the story was prefixed to them at a later stage, in the way that prose narratives have been prefixed to verses in the Itivuttaka and Udāna, for instance. The reiterated refrain, '*tādisaṃ bhikkhum āsajja kaṇha dukkhaṃ nigacchasi*', with its constant reference to the idea that for striking a monk who understands such and such a truth (the truths which are set out in the verses), Kaṇha is bound to suffer, recalls the idea found in the Ātānāṭiya Sutta, that a yakkha who attacks a follower of the Buddha will be punished (D III. 204).

A curious feature of these verses is the exclusive use of the name Kaṇha throughout the first forty lines. This is rather remarkable if the verses were from the beginning of their history always understood as referring to Māra; it is unusual for Māra to be addressed so regularly and exclusively by an alternative appellation, without any use whatever of the more customary 'Māra' or 'pāpimā'. But this feature of the verses becomes intelligible when it is recalled that there is a tradition, attested in the Dīgha Nikāya, that *kaṇha* is an ancient synonym for *pisāca*, or fiend. (see D.I. 93). These verses, moreover, addressed thus regularly to some demonic creature called a kaṇha have all the appearance of an animistic protective chant or *paritta*, of which there are other examples in the Pāḷi Canon. Only in the last eight lines is the name Māra introduced, and this, together with the considerations just mentioned, suggests that the relation of these last eight lines to the preceding forty may well be that of an epilogue added later when the verses were brought into use in the sutta's present form, in connexion with the Māra mythology. In this use of the verses the word *kaṇha* becomes '*Kaṇha*'—that is, a proper name, an alternative name, for Māra. There is thus possibly evidence in this sutta of the way in which material which originally related to common feature of the popular demonology could be pressed into the service of the Māra mythology without undue difficulty.

The exordium, concerning Moggallāna's encounter with Māra, is complete in the form in which it stands (up to the point where Māra, being recognized, is driven out; this would have been a fairly usual kind of ending for a simple story of the kind which is found in the Māra-Saṃyutta). Such a story would have illustrated the point, dealt with over and over again in similar episodes, that Māra, when recognized, is defeated. Taken as a whole, therefore, this sutta in its present compound form, may well be regarded as an illustration of the way in which the legendary material concerning Māra gradually received didactic accretions, until the didactic element became predominant.

(III) The third element of the Māra material in this Nikāya is, now, to be considered; this is the purely didactic material, which, in the Majjhima, consists mainly of parables, with their appended expositions.

1. The first of these is the parable of the deer, found in the *Dvedhāvitakka Sutta* (M I. 114 ff.). This sutta contains an account by the Buddha of the events that occurred during the

night of his Enlightenment, followed immediately by the parable.

This tells how once there was a herd of deer living near a large area of marshy ground in a forest grove; there came a man who, by blocking up the one road that was secure, safe and pleasant to walk on, and by tethering a male and female decoy deer, succeeded in leading the herd away to the dangerous ground. But there then came also a man desiring their good, who opened up that road that was secure and pleasant, and sent away the decoys, so that the herd might increase and prosper once more.

The interpretation of the parable follows: The marshy ground represents the sense-pleasures; the herd of deer are 'beings' (*sattā*); the man not desiring their good is Māra the Evil One. The treacherous way by which he leads them is the eightfold wrong path; the male decoy is the passion of delight (*nandirāga*) and the female decoy is *avijjā*. The man who desires their good is the Tathāgata, the arahat, the *sammāsambuddha*; the way that is secure and safe and pleasant is the holy eightfold path. The interpretation of the parable ends with the reminder that what is to be done out of compassion by a Teacher seeking the welfare of his disciples has been done by the Buddha for his followers; there is a final exhortation to the bhikkhus to meditate and not to be slothful, that they may not afterwards experience remorse: '*Jhāyatha, bhikkhave, mā pamādattha, mā pacchā vippaṭisārino ahuvattha.*' (M I. 118.)

It will be observed that the parable assumes that there is a direct opposition and contrast between Māra and the Buddha. It must be noted also that *avijjā* is a decoy, an agent used by Māra.

2. Another parable of this kind is found in the *Nivāpa Sutta* (M I. 151 ff.), the parable of the crops. This starts from the statement that a sower would be unlikely to sow crops for deer to come and eat, simply in order that they might flourish, but rather that having enticed them to his ground, he might do with them as he wished. Four successive herds of deer are then described. First came a herd which ate, and grew careless and was captured. A second herd, noting what had happened to the first, held back and retired to the forest. But in the course of time hunger made them weak, and they were forced to come again to the crops; they too then ate, and grew careless, and were captured. The third herd of deer, noting what had happened

to the previous two, made a lair near the field, in which to hide from the sower and his men, and from which they could sally forth and feed whenever the sower was not about. But by and by their lair was discovered, and they too were captured. Finally, the fourth herd, observing all this, decided to make a lair in a place where the sower and his men could not come (*agati*) (literally, where there was 'no-coming' or 'non-access' for them; *agati* is often used in this way in connexion with Māra). When the sower had observed this he decided to leave those deer alone, lest they should communicate with others, and he should lose all his quarry. So the fourth herd lived without interference from the sower and his men. Again, the interpretation of the parable follows: The crops are the five strands of sense-pleasures (*kāmaguṇā*). The sower is Māra the Evil One. The sower's men are Māra's retinue (*Māra-parisā*). The herds of deer are various kinds of recluses and holy men. The first herd are those who quickly fall victims to the delights of material things, those to be done to by Māra as he wills, there amid his crops, amid worldly baits (*lokāmise*). The second herd are those recluses and holy men who, realizing the danger from Māra, refrain from the enjoyment of material things for a time, but then, when their bodies become emaciated, are forced back again upon material things; now, however, with freedom of mind impaired, having once begun to eat they go quickly to excess and fall victims to Māra. The third are they who realizing what has happened to the others determine to partake of material things without becoming infatuated with them, and therefore make provision for the necessary withdrawal from the enjoyment of material pleasures. These also, however, are attacked by Māra, he is able to reach them because they hold definite views (*diṭṭhi*) about the world, about the life-principle, about the body, and so on. Finally the fourth herd are those recluses and holy men who, understanding the dangers into which their predecessors have fallen, make their abode where there is no access for Māra and his retinue (*Yattha agati Mārassa ca Māraparisāya ca* . . . (M I. 158).

The rest of the discourse in then devoted to this subject of abiding where there is '*agati Mārassa*', non-access for Māra. This is identified with abiding in the first, second, third and fourth *jhānas*, and with passing beyond the *jhānas* into the plane called *ākāsānañcayatana*, thence to *viññāṇañcāyatana*, and thence to *ākiñcaññāyātana* thence to *nevasaññānāsaññāyatana*, and finally to *saññāvedayitanirodha*. There is thus a clear relationship between meditation and the overcoming of Māra. After each of the foregoing nine stages of meditation the comment occurs: this monk is called one who has made Māra blind, who, having cut off Māra's vision, goes unseen by the Evil One; after the ninth repetition of this comment are added the words: he has crossed over the world's flood (*tiṇṇo loke vissattikaṁ*.)

This discourse provides a good example of Theravāda teaching concerning the way to safety from Māra, indicating how closely associated is the theme of escape from Māra with the practice of meditation.

3. A further similar parable is found in the next sutta, No. 26, the *Ariyapariyesana Sutta* (M I. 160 ff.). The Buddha is warning the group of five bhikkhus about the danger of infatuation and enslavement by the five sense-pleasures, for, he declares, these put one under the mastery of the Evil One. He who becomes thus infatuated is like a deer in a forest caught in a snare, of whom it would be said: 'It has come to calamity .... it is one to be done to by the trapper as he wills ... '. But he who experiences the five sense-pleasures without becoming infatuated by them is like a deer in a forest which lies down upon a snare but is not caught in it; when the trapper comes, it will be able to go away as it wishes; so such a one is not mastered by the Evil One. Like a deer in a forest who roams confidently because it is out of the trapper's reach, so is he who enters into and abides in the first *jhāna*; he has made Māra blind, he has cut off Māra's vision and goes unseen by the Evil One. The sequence of nine stages is followed through as in the previous parable and the comment about blinding Māra is added after each stage.

4. In the *Cūḷagopālaka Sutta* (M I. 225 ff.) it is said by the Buddha that recluses and holy men who are unskilled about this world, the world beyond, about Māra's realm (*Māradheyya*) and what is not Māra's realm, about Death's realm (*Maccudheyya*) and what is not Death's realm, are like an incompetent cowherd who drove his cattle across the Ganges at the end of the rainy season at a place where there was no ford; those who listen to such recluses and holy men are like his cattle. (M I. 225). According to the commentary, *Māradheyya* is to be understood

as a comprehensive term for the threefold becoming, *Kāma-*, *rūpa-*, and *arūpa-* (M A II. 266). Similarly, those on the other hand who are skilled about all these matters are like a competent cowherd who took his cattle across in safety and good order, at a place where there was a ford; they who heed such teachers are, again, like the cattle; of them it is said that they cut across Māra's stream and go safely beyond. (The Pāli commentator says at this point that this means: beyond *saṃsāra* to *nibbāna*. M A II. 267). Such a teacher, it is then affirmed, is the Buddha, skilled about this world, the world beyond, Māra's realm, and what is not Māra's realm, Death's realm and what is not Death's realm. The separate allusions to Māra and to Maccu might be thought to indicate that two separate beings are meant. However, in the verses with which the sutta closes these two symbols are, so to speak, telescoped:

> This world, the world beyond, are well explained by the one who knows,
> And what is accessible to Māra, and what is not accessible *to* Death (*Maccu*) (M I. 227).

In these closing verses support is found also for the commentator's equating of Māra's stream with *saṃsāra*, and of what lies beyond that stream with *nibbāna*:

> *vivaṭaṁ amatadvāraṃ khemaṃ nibbānapattiyā*
> *chinnaṃ pāpimato sotaṃ viddhastaṃ vinaḷīkataṃ*
> (M I. 227).

A further reference to sense pleasures and the perception of them as constituting Māra's realm is found in the Āṇañjasappāya Sutta (M. II. 261 ff.). Perhaps with the other parables in mind, the sense pleasures are spoken of as not only as *Māradheyya*, but also as Māra's crop (*Mārassa nivāpa*), Māra's sphere (*Mārassa visayo*), Māra's pasturage (*Mārassa gocara*). (M II. 262).

The importance of mindfulness (*sati*) in connection with security from Māra is mentioned again in the Kāyagatāsati Sutta (M III. 88 ff). Here it is said that Māra gains access to any bhikkhu in whom mindfulness of body has not been developed—just as a heavy stone thrown into a mound of moist clay would have an easy entrance, just as easily as a dry stick is ignited and burns, just as easily as a load of water can fill an empty water pot, so easily does Māra gain access to such a bhikkhu. The statement is then made and illustrated in the reverse form: as impossible as it would be for a ball of thread thrown against a wooden door to penetrate the door, as impossible as it is to ignite a wet, sappy stick, as impossible as it is to fill an already full water pot, just so completely is Māra repelled from the bhikkhu in whom mindfulness of body is developed.

A final reference belonging to the same kind of teaching about Māra may be noted from the Mahāsuññata Sutta (M III. 109 ff.). Certain 'states' are being described (*dhammā ekantakusalāyatikā*). These states, it is said, which are concerned solely with what is skilled, are ariyan, are supermundane, are beyond the range of the Evil One: '*Ime kho te, Ānanda, dhammā ekantakusalāyatikā ariyā lokuttarā anavakkhantāpāpimatā*' (M III. 115).

The equation of the three terms *ariya lokuttara* and *anavakkhantāpāpimatā* is of special interest. *Ariya* refers to that which is specifically Buddhist, *lokuttara* is a common synonym for Nibbāna, that which transcends the three spheres into which the universe was divided in Indian cosmology; Nibbāna, in this sense, is also a specifically Buddhist conception. Hence, going beyond the range of the Evil One is regarded as belonging together with those things which are *specifically Buddhist.*

3 AṄGUTTARA NIKĀYA

(1) In this Nikāya, as in the two previous, the name Māra occurs fairly regularly in conventional descriptive formulas. The following examples are found.

The connexion between a 'vision' of the world, with all its supernatural and its human creatures, and the experience of Enlightenment, is attested again, in the words: '*abbhaññāsiṃ athāham . . . sadevake loke samārake* . . . etc. (A I. 259); *so imaṃ lokaṃ sadevakaṃ samārakaṃ* . . . etc. . . . *abhiññā sacchikatvā pavedeti*' (A III. 30; IV. 56). Such vision, as the Buddha's way of seeing the world, is the most frequent context in which the formula occurs: *nāhan taṃ brāhmaṇa passāmi sadevake loke samārake* etc. . . . (A IV. 173; V. 48; see also II. 9; II. 171; III. 54 (3 times); III. 57; III. 148; III. 346; IV. 83; IV. 259 and IV. 304).

(II) *Māra: Legendary references*

The Māra material of a legendary nature is, in this Nikāya, confined to the somewhat abbreviated version of the Parinibbāna Sutta (A IV. 308 ff.) which is found here. The legend in the same form in which it is found in the Dīgha Nikāya is followed here up to the point at which the Buddha, after his statement to Māra that he will pass away in three months' time, renounces his right to live to the end of the *kappa*; at this, a great earthquake arose, and Ānanda, upon his coming and asking the reason for its occurrence is instructed by the Buddha in the eight natural and psychic causes for such a phenomenon. Since the account is found in the Aṭṭhaka Nipāta it is evident that these *eight* reasons for an earthquake, the majority of which have to do with the marvellous powers of the Tathāgata etc., are the crux of the matter; what has been related up to this point leads up to the mention of these eight reasons. There is no further mention of Māra. This version of the Parinibbāna narrative thus adds nothing to what has already been noted except that it shows how integral to the story is the detail about Māra, and his approaching the Buddha on the subject of his parinibbāna; the narrative in this case could equally well have started from the point when, at the shrine of Capala, the Buddha cast aside the sum of life, and there arose a great earthquake; this would have been just as effective in introducing the eight reasons. Nevertheless the legend is recounted from the beginning, and the Māra details are an indispensable element of the narrative.

(III) *Didactic references to Māra*

1. The connexion between Māra and death receives emphasis in the verse found at the conclusion of sutta 40 of the *Tika Nipāta*:

Dhammādhipo ca anudhammacārī
na hīyati saccaparakkamo muni
Pasayha Māraṃ abhibhuyya antakaṃ
So ca phusī jātikkhayaṃ padhānavā

(A I. 150).

The last two lines will be seen to be a threefold expression of the same fact: Māra is conquered = death is vanquished = the round of rebirths is ended. This is one of many such passages in the Sutta Piṭaka where this connexion is affirmed. Māra is associated with death, but death is not simply the event which terminates the individual life; it is rather the preliminary to inevitable further karmic existence. It is this which gives the death of the unenlightened man its dread aspect, to be subject to *karmic rebirth*.

2. This idea occurs again in sutta thirteen of the Catukka-Nipāta. (A II. 15 f.) The 'four right efforts' (*sammāppadhānāni*) are the subject of the discourse (described also in the Dīgha, II. 120 and the Majjhima II. 11 and elsewhere). As they are described here they consist of (*i*) avoiding evil states not yet arisen; (*ii*) overcoming evil states that have arisen; (*iii*) developing good states not yet arisen; and (*iv*) maintaining those that have arisen. After this account of the four right efforts, the sutta closes with a sloka about the overcoming of Māra's realm.

> 'By right exertion (*sammāppadhānā*) they have conquered Māra's realm (*Māradheyyādhibhuno*)
> Freed they have passed beyond the fear of birth and death (*jātimaraṇabhayassa pāragū*)
> These happy ones have vanquished Māra and his mount (*Māraṃ savāhanaṃ*)
> And from all power of Namuci escaping are in bliss'
> (A II. 15).

Once again, Māra's realm is identified with birth and death, and here the way of rising out of it, (adhibhavati) becoming superior to it, is by sammappadhāna—one of the steps of the holy eightfold path, and one whose positive features, as they are described in the next suttas, included such elements of enlightenment as *viriya, sati* and *samādhi* (see sutta 14, Catukka-N.) (A II. 16 f.).

The occurrence of the name Namuci is of interest, since here it is evidently used as a synonym for Māra, and not for another demon as in the Dīgha Nikāya. This suggests that this sutta represents a stage in the development of the mythology at which the two figures, Namuci and Māra, had coalesced.

3. A somewhat unusual reference to Māra occurs in sutta 15 of the Catukka-Nipāta (A II. 17). Here four types of beings are listed; they are as follows: chief of those who have personality is Rāhu lord of asuras (*etadaggam attabhāvīnaṃ yadidaṃ*

Rāhu asurindo); chief of those who are given to sense-pleasure (*kāmabhogīnaṁ*) is Mandhātā-rājā; chief of these who have lordship (*adhipateyyānam*) is Māra the Evil One; chief among all beings in the world of gods and men (*sadevake loke sāmarake sabrahmake* etc.—the conventional comprehensive cosmic formula), is the Tathāgata, the Arahat, the sammāsambuddha. A curious feature of this list is that lordship of those who are given to sense-pleasures is ascribed to Mandhātā, rather that to Māra. Mandhātā is mentioned in the Jātakas also (II. 310; III. 454), and in the Milindapañha (115) and the Therīgāthā (485). He is said to be king of the world's four continents, and a mythical ancestor of the Sakiya people. The fact that Māra is, in this context, described as chief of those that have lordship (*ādhipateyyānaṃ*) may indicate that he is to be understood as Mandhātā's superior; or conversely, that Mandhātā, as lord of sense-pleasure, is a subordinate officer to Māra. This likelihood is strengthened by the evident progression in importance in the hierarchy, as they are described in the concluding verses, where half a line each is allowed to the first two, Rāhu and Mandhātā; a line to Māra, and two lines to the Buddha. This idea of Māra as a 'chief of the powers' (*ādhipateyyā*) is noteworthy, in view of the similar status ascribed to the Devil in Ephesians 6, where the *archai*, *exousiai*, etc. are implicitly regarded as under the direction of *ho diabolos*.

4. A reference to Māra and 'his mount' was noted in sutta 13 of the Catukka-N. Another such reference is found in sutta 16 of the same Nipāta. Here it is said that the bhikkhu who 'sees' aright (*sammaddaso*) bears his final body (that is, is no longer subject to karmic rebirth), 'since he has conquered Māra and his mount' (*jetvā Māraṃ savāhanaṃ*) (A II. 18). The picture is one of a warrior riding into battle mounted on his elephant, and is an example of the more concrete kind of imagery in which the Māra mythology is often presented in the Suttapiṭaka.

5. In sutta 49 of the Catukka-Nipāta (A II. 52) it is said that those who hold perverse views are bond-slaves to Māra. Examples of such perverse views are mentioned: to see in change that which is permanent; to see happiness in what is ill; to see the self in what is not the self; and to see the fair in what is foul. Māra's interest in the upholding of false views was noticed in the Majjhima Nikāya (Mūlapaṇṇāsa Su). There it was said that

a false view (*idaṁ niccaṁ*, etc.) was the outcome of *avijjā*, and Māra was represented as protecting the propagation of such views and resisting any denial of them. Here it is simply said that those who hold such views are Māra's slaves.

6. The idea that womanhood constitutes, for the bhikkhu, Māra's snare is fairly common to the Sutta-Piṭaka. An instance of this occurs in sutta 55 of the Pañcaka Nipāta. 'Womanhood is wholly a snare of Māra' (A III. 68).

The deadly nature of this 'snare' is evident from the verse (A III. 69), which says that it would be better for a bhikkhu to parley with a man with a sword in hand, better to dispute with a fiend, better to sit close to an envenomed snake, than to talk alone with a woman.

7. Sutta No. 60 of the Sattaka-Nipāta concludes with some verses describing the wrathful man. They who act in wrath, it is said, perceive not that their deeds bring Maccu's snare.

Bhūnahaccāni kammāni attamāraṇiyāni ca
Karontā nāvabujjanti kodhajāto parābhavo
Itāyaṃ kodharūpena maccupāso guhāsayo
(A IV. 98).

8. Sutta 63 of the same Nipāta, (A IV. 106 ff.) entitled Nāgaraṇi, consists of a lengthy parable, similar to those noted in the Majjhima, and followed by its exposition. A rajah's citadel is described; it possesses the seven requisites of a fortress and four kinds of supplies necessary for the well-being of its inhabitants; it is therefore of the kind 'that cannot be undone by outside foe or perfidious ally'. The seven requisites, or varieties of protection, are then described one by one. First is the pillar (at the centre), which, being unmovable, unshakable is the symbol of stability; the second is the moat; the third is the road encircling the citadel; the fourth is the armoury; the fifth the body of troops; the sixth the wise gatekeeper, refusing entrance to the unknown; and the seventh is the rampart, high and wide, for warding off attackers. The four kinds of supplies are the various kinds of stores and provisions—grass, wood and water; corn; vegetables; and miscellaneous foods.

Similarly it is said the disciple (*ariyasāvaka*) who possesses the seven kinds of protection or seven 'good things' (*saddhammā*), and the four kinds of supplies or meditations (jhānā) may be described as one who cannot be undone by Māra the Evil One.

The seven saddhammā are then described in greater detail. They are: first, like the pillar which renders the fortress unshakable, faith (*saddha*), which consists of belief in the Tathāgata's enlightenment. Second is the moat, that is, the disciple's conscientiousness (*ariyasāvako hirimā hoti*) which protects him against misconduct and evil ways. Third, like the citadel is the disciple's fear of blame (*ariyasāvako ottappī hoti*). Fourth, like the citadel's great armoury of sword and spear is the disciple's store of things heard, that is, the *Dhamma*, which he has learnt and made familiar, pondered over, and penetrated by 'right-view'. As the fifth item the disciple has 'energy' (*viriya*) as an armed force. The sixth defence, the wise gatekeeper of the citadel, is mindfulness (*sati*), and the seventh, the rampart for warding off intruders, is vision (*paññā*).

The four 'good things', which like the supplies for the inmates of the citadel, bring comfort and well-being to the disciple, are the four jhānas. In this way it is emphasized that to enjoy a state of well-being, safe from attack by Māra, the disciple must be possessed of the seven qualities mentioned, while the nourishment of the life lived within the protection of these qualities is afforded by his entering and abiding in the four jhānas.

9. The notion of putting oneself beyond the influence of Māra's sway is found again in sutta 29 of the Aṭṭhaka-Nipāta. (A IV. 225 f.). Those who walk in the way declared by the Tathāgata are said to have cut off all 'tendencies' or 'inclinations' (*anusaye*) which follow in the wake of Māra's influence; they will reach the world beyond with all *āsavas* destroyed.

> *Sabbe anusaye chetvā Māradheyyasarānuge*
> *te ve pāragatā loke ye pattā āsavakkhayan ti*
>
> (A IV. 228).

10. Finally, there is a reference to Māra in a passage which has already been noticed in another connexion. This is the sutta describing the battles between the devas and the asuras (Navaka-Nipāta sutta 39. A IV 432 ff.) in which in turn first the asuras and then the devas are victorious and retire to their own stronghold, in order to have no further

dealings with their adversaries. The myth is then used as an illustration of how a bhikkhu should enter into and abide in the jhānas, as a refuge where he will no longer have any dealings with Māra. In abiding thus in the jhānas he is said to have put a darkness about Māra and Māra's vision (*bhikkhu antaṃ akāsi Māraṃ apadaṃ vadhitvā Māracakkhuṃ adassanaṃ gato pāpimato tiṇṇo loke vissatikan ti*) (A IV. 434). The idea that he who meditates in this way, abiding in the jhānas, has escaped Māra's range of vision, has already been encountered in the Majjhima Nikāya.

4 SAṂYUTTA NIKĀYA

(I) Conventional formulas. The conventional cosmic formulas in which reference is made to Māra are found here in a similar form to those found in other Nikāyas. There is, however, a variation of this form to be found here which has not been encountered in previous Nikāyas. The usual context for this, as it occurs in the Saṃyutta Nikāya, is a passage in which the Buddha is comparing his lack of insight into the nature of the world before he was enlightened with what he was able to discern after that event. Before my enlightenment, he says, *neva tāvāham bhikkhave sadevake loke samārake sabrahmake sassamaṇabrahmaṇiyā pajāya sadevamanussāya anuttaraṃ sammāsambodhim abhisambuddho ti paccaññāsiṃ*. But, after my enlightenment, *athāham bhikkhave sadevake loke samārake . . . abhisambuddho ti paccaññāsim* (S II. 170). Other occurrences of this form of expression are at S III. 28; 30; IV. 158; V 204; 423.

It is evident that the insight which sees the world with its devas, its Māra, its Brahmā, its recluses and brahmins, is supernatural insight. This is already inferred in previous examples of the conventional formula that have been examined, in the use of *abhiññā*, as the verb form governing the whole range of items. It is noteworthy in this connexion that the epithet 'world-knower' (*loka-vidu*), which in the Dīgha is applied to the Buddha Maitreya, is in the Saṃyutta Nikāya applied to the *arahat* also (S I. 62; V. 197; 343; etc.). The special significance of this point was noted in Chap. 3 (p. 49 f) when the Māra references as a whole were considered. It is enough at this stage to notice the clear indication which is given by the form of the conventional expression used here that the object of the supernatural insight is the nature of the world, with its Māra, its Brahmā etc.

(II) *Legendary material*

The Māra Saṃyutta. This collection of suttas, together with the Bhikkhunī suttas which immediately follow them in the Saṃyutta Nikāya, constitutes the largest single block of material for the Māra legend in the Pāli Canon. The suttas describe actual approaches of Māra to the Buddha, and to the bhikkhus and bhikkhunīs, but at the same time these stories about Māra do also convey indirectly a good deal of teaching about Māra and his ways, and are in that sense didactic also.

In the Māra-Saṃyutta there are three groups of suttas; the first two have ten suttas each and the third has five. The Bhikkhunī-Saṃyutta is a group of ten. There is thus here a block of thirty-five suttas devoted to the legend of Māra. This fact in itself testifies to the prominence which the Māra symbol had in early Buddhism.

While these suttas provide valuable evidence of the quantity of material which existed about Māra's attempts to assail the Buddha and his followers, they do not, however, provide a complete account of the early Buddhist Māra legend. That is to say, if these suttas only had survived, certain important features of the legend would be missing. For the Māra-Saṃyutta relates to the period immediately after the Sammāsambodhi, and the years of the Buddha's itinerant preaching that followed. From the position of the Sattavassāni Sutta nearly at the end of Vagga III, it seems likely that these suttas deal with the first six years of preaching (the 'seven years', according to the Pāli commentator, being understood as one before and six after the Bodhi).

As these suttas have so many common elements, it will be convenient first to deal with those features which are characteristic of the collection as a whole, and then to note particular points of interest which arise within the individual suttas.

The pattern of the suttas. This is virtually the same in every case; the last two suttas of the third vagga being of a special nature (*Sattavassāni*, and *Dhītaro*). This common pattern contains the following features:

A The locality is named.
B The circumstances are described; i.e. what the Buddha, or the bhikkhu concerned, was doing.
C The approach of Māra, with some hostile purpose which is either stated or implied.
D Māra speaks (or acts).
E Suitable rejoinder is made.
F Māra retires, foiled and discomfited.

In order to provide an adequate summary of the contents of these suttas it is necessary to give a somewhat expanded account of each of the items in this pattern.

A and *B* may be dealt with jointly: that is, the location and occasion, and circumstances of the person or persons involved. The following table shows the variety of places and circumstances which the legend covers in these suttas:

Sutta	I. *Place*	II. *Person(s) approached by Māra*	III *Circumstances*	IV. *Māra addressed as:*
I. 1.	Uruvelā	Buddha	Meditating alone	*Antaka*
I. 2.	Uruvelā	Buddha	Meditating alone (night)	*Pāpimā* *Antaka*
I. 3.	Uruvelā	Buddha	Meditating alone (night)	*Pāpimā* *Antaka* *Māra*
I. 4.	Isipatana	Buddha	Addressing bhikkhus	*Māra* *Antaka*
I. 5.	Isipatana	Buddha	Addressing bhikkhus	*Antaka*
I. 6.	Rājagaha	Buddha	Meditating alone (night)	—
I. 7.	Rājagaha	Buddha	Preparing for sleep (towards dawn)	*Māra*
I. 9.	Sāvatthī	Buddha	—	—
I. 9.	Rājagaha	Buddha	Addressing bhikkhus	—
I. 10.	Rājagaha	Buddha	Addressing bhikkhus	—
II. 1.	Rājagaha	Buddha	Meditating alone (night)	
II. 2.	Sāvatthī	Buddha	Addressing large gathering	—
II. 3.	Rājagaha	Buddha	Alone	—
II. 4.	Ekasālā	Buddha	Addressing large gathering	—

Sutta	I. Place	II. Person(s) approached by Māra	III. Circumstances	IV. Māra addressed as:
II. 5.	Sāvatthī	Buddha	Alone	—
II. 6.	Sāvatthī	Bhikkhus	Buddha addressing bhikkhus	(*Māra*) (Pāpimā)
II. 7.	Vesālī	Bhikkhus	Buddha addressing bhikkhus	(*Māra*) (Pāpimā)
II. 8.	Pañcasālā	a. Brahman householders	Buddha on alms-round	*Pāpimā*
		b. Buddha		*Māra* *Pāpimā*
II. 9.	Sāvatthī	Bhikkhus	Buddha addressing bhikkhus	*Pāpimā* *Pāpimā*
II. 10.	Kosala	Buddha	Meditating alone	*Pāpimā*
III. 1.	Silavātī	Bhikkhus	Bhikkhus abiding self-resolute, etc.	(Māra) (Pāpimā)
III. 2.	Silavātī	Samiddhi	Samiddhi abiding self-resolute, etc.	(Māra) (Pāpimā)
III. 3.	Rājagaha	Buddha	Godhika dies at his own hand	(Māra) (Pāpimā)
III. 4.	Uruvelā	Buddha	Meditating alone	*Pamatta-bandhu* Pāpimā
III. 5.	[? as III. 4]	Buddha	Meditating alone	—

From this analysis of the suttas, several observations may be made:

1. In most of the suttas it is the Buddha whom Māra approaches (20 out of 25 cases)

2. More often than not, the Buddha is alone when Māra approaches him (13 out of 20 cases)

3. These attempts to assail the Buddha are not confined to any one place, such as Uruvelā, for example. This appears to indicate either, as Windisch suggested, the widespread geographical extent over which these legends were known and narrated originally, or else an intention to demonstrate from the life of the Buddha that Māra may be encountered everywhere.

4. There is a similar variety of occasions on which Māra makes his approach: when the Buddha is alone, or when surrounded by bhikkhus whom he is instructing, or when he is

addressing a large gathering, when he is on his alms-round, or when he is preparing for sleep. Similarly in the five cases where Māra approaches bhikkhus, sometimes it is when they are alone, sometimes it is when the Buddha is instructing them. The times of Māra's approach also vary: the middle of the night (I. 2, 3, 6, II. 1),[1] towards dawn (I. 7), the early morning (II. 8) etc. One thus learns from these suttas that Māra may make his approach at any time of day or night.

5. Column IV shows the various names that are used in referring to the Evil One. Italics indicate that its name occurs in the verses. Brackets indicate an indirect allusion in the third person.

The results of this analysis are as follows. The Evil One is apostrophized:

as Pāpimā — 7 times
as Antaka — 6 times
as Māra — 4 times

All of these occur in the verses, except three instances of Pāpimā, which are in the narrative. The verses may possibly represent more primitive material. There is thus much to be said for Windisch's view that it was primarily as Death that Māra was thought of—Death as the great Ill. The significance of this point was considered on p. 65.

C. Some hostile purpose always lies behind Māra's approach, whether this is actually mentioned in the sutta, or only implied. Sometimes it is to inspire terror into the Buddha, (I. 2; 3; 6; II. 1) or into the bhikkhus, in order to cause confusion (II. 7; III. 2). Sometimes it is to reproach the Buddha (I. 7), or to correct him (I. 1), or to confuse his hearers (II. 2; 4. 6. 9). In short, Māra's purpose is usually either to interrupt the Buddha's or the Bhikkhus' meditation, or to interfere with the Buddha's preaching. It will also be noted that not infrequently Māra assumes a disguise: for example; a king-elephant (*mahantaṃ hatthirājavaṇṇaṃ*) I. 2; a king-snake (*mahantaṃ sapparājavaṇṇaṃ*) I. 6; divers visible shapes, beautiful and ugly (*uccāvacā vaṇṇanibhā . . . subhā c'eva asubhā ca*) I. 3; a bullock, II. 6; a ploughman, II. 9; and a brahmin, III. 1.

D. Sometimes Māra tries to assail his victim by means of what might be described as terrible physical phenomena such

[1] References here are to the vaggas and sutta numbers of the Māra-Saṃyutta.

as a landslide (II. 1) or an earthquake (II. 7). But more usually he draws near and addresses him (*upasankamitvā Bhagavantaṃ gāthāya ajjhabhāsi* is the usual wording.) In what he says Māra almost always reveals his own lack of knowledge of the true situation. Thus although the Buddha refers more than once to his own immunity from Māra's attacks (*mutto-ham Mārapāsena* .... I. 4; *patto-smi paramaṃ suddhiṃ* I. 1), again and again Māra appears entirely unable to realize this or to accept it, until the final sutta (*Dhītaro*), in which at last he is represented as recognizing the extreme difficulty of capturing the Buddha: '*Arahaṃ sugato loke na rāgena suvānayo* ...' Certainly he is not 'easy to bring' (*su—anaya*), by the ordinary means of passion or lust (rāga), and Māra tells his daughters they are wasting their time; the Arahat will not thus be captured.

E. The rejoinder to Māra is, in these suttas, usually made by the Buddha, or at his instructions, as in the case of Samiddhi (III. 2). The Buddha is always, without exception, aware of Māra's presence and of his intentions. Whatever disguises Māra may assume, the Buddha recognizes him. In the five suttas where bhikkhus are the objects of Māra's attention, it is again the Buddha who recognizes the Evil One's presence. The reply to Māra therefore usually includes some reference to his unmasking or humiliation. A common form of words used is, '*nihato tvaṃ asi, antaka*'.

F. Almost invariably the sutta ends with the doleful refrain chanted by Māra, as he retires thwarted; '*Jānāti maṃ Bhagavā* ....' Even in the case of Samiddhi, where this takes the form '*Jānāti maṃ Samiddhi bhikkhu* ...' this is because Samiddhi has been instructed by the Buddha ('*N'esa Samiddhi pathavī udrīyati. Māra eso pāpimā tuyhaṃ vicakkhukammāya āgato* ...') It is noteworthy that in the one case where Māra approaches some brahmin householders (II. 8), he is entirely successful, and there is no suggestion that they have any awareness then or subsequently, of the presence of the machinations of Māra. This points to the conclusion which the reader or hearer of these suttas cannot fail to reach, that Māra is recognized and ousted only by the one who is *Sammāsambuddha*, or by those who, by his insight, have had Māra's presence revealed to them.

Some specific points within the suttas may now be noted.

I. 1. (*Tapo kammañ ca*) Emphasis is laid upon the fact that he who is about to be approached by Māra is the fully awakened, the Liberated: *pathamābhisambuddho . . . mutto . . . sādhu mutto . . . sato, bodhiṃ samajjhagaṃ.* Māra's method is seen to consist of an attempt to confuse the Buddha by casting doubts upon his newly won purification, and by trying to persuade him that it exists only in his own imagination:

asuddho maññati suddho
suddhimaggam aparaddho

It is also to be noted that Māra appears as the representative and defender of the traditional ascetic forms of religion (*tapo-kamma*).

I. 2. The phrase *bhayaṃ chambhittattaṃ lomahaṃsaṃ uppādetukāmo* links Māra with the yakkha mythology (in view of the same phrase, for example, applied to a yakkha, at Ud 5). It could be that the yakkha mythology has been influenced by the Māra legend; which is historically prior is a matter of less importance for the present study than fact that Māra stories and yakkha stories can share common features.

The various guises in which Māra appears may be either attractive or repulsive: *saṃsāraṃ dīgham addhānam vaṇṇam katvā subhāsubham.*

I. 3. The guises of Māra are again mentioned, and again their variety is emphasized: *uccāvacā vaṇṇanibhā upadaṃseti subhā c-eva asubhā ca.*

I. 4, 5. Māra's words to the Buddha, spoken directly and without any attempt at dissimulation, are worthy of note: *na me samaṇa mokkhasi.* The hearer of the sutta would recognize this as patently untrue; he who is Buddha has escaped already. It may therefore be inferred that Māra is simply speaking a lie in an attempt to produce doubts in the mind of his opponent. The alternative explanation, is that Māra cannot understand the possibility of anyone finally escaping from his power. The evidence of the Māra-Saṃyutta would appear at least to be that it takes Māra some considerable time to accept this fact, but nevertheless, finally (as recorded in the Satta-vassāni Sutta), he does appear to acknowledge himself beaten. Here, however, in suttas 4 and 5, Māra has not yet sunk to that depth of dejection; he is, if at all, only dimly aware of the Buddha's newly won release. Whichever explanation of his words here is adopted, whether it is from malice or from ignorance, Māra's voice is represented as the voice of untruth.

I. 7. The gātha spoken by the Buddha is of special interest in that certain important abstract terms are found in conjunction with the mythological term 'Māra' in a verse which is of a relatively primitive nature:

Yassa jālinī visattikā
taṇhā n'atthi kuhiñci netave
sabbūpadhīnam parikkhayā buddho
soppati kin-tav-ettha Mārā ti.

The infinitive *netave* is, according to Geiger, a Vedic form which is confined to Gāthā-language (PLL, p. 224). This would appear to indicate that the gātha is relatively early. It is therefore of some interest to notice that *taṇhā* and *upadhi* (as the substrate of rebirth) are mentioned in the same context as Māra in a manner which makes it clear that from early times Māra was conceived to have a special connexion with them.

I. 8. The gātha spoken by Māra here (*Nandati puttehi puttimā* etc) is found also in the Deva-suttas (2. 1), and in the Sutta Nipāta (Sn 33). In the former case the words are spoken by a deva; and in the latter by Māra, where, spoken without warning, in a conversation between the Buddha and Dhaniya the rich herdsman, the effect would doubtless be to suggest that these are the words of the ordinary man; they are spoken from the 'common-sense' point of view. That they represent a popular sentiment is sufficiently attested by their appearance in these three different places in the Suttas. To attribute them to Māra, here and in the Sn, is an indication that it was understood among early Buddhists that the 'common-sense' point of view might very well be Māra-inspired: Māra's hall-mark is not necessarily that which is patently evil.

The same kind of understanding is indicated in the next two suttas also, I. 9 and 10 (*Āyu*), in which Māra speaks words which appear to represent the unreflective attitude of the ordinary person:

Dīgham āyu manussānam, na nam hīle suporiso
careyya khīramatto va natthi maccussa āgamo ti
(9)

Nāccayanti ahorattā, jīvitaṃ n'uparujjhati
āyu anupariyāti maccānam, nemi va ratha-kubbaran-ti
(10)

II. 1. The presence of Māra is recognized by the Buddha in the kind of phenomenon which would be likely to inspire terror into an ordinary mortal—a crashing down of huge rocks in the darkness of the night. More important for the present study is the fact that if any explanation for such a happening were offered by the Buddha's contemporaries it would be that this was the work of a Yakkha, or some similar creature, since these were generally regarded as the agents of all uncanny and frightening occurrences. Where the ordinary man accounted for such an experience in terms of yakkhas, the Buddha is represented as discerning the presence of Māra. And whereas the response of the ordinary man would be one of terror, because he felt himself in the presence of such terrifying and hostile yakkhas, the Buddha, by contrast, is entirely unmoved. He points out to Māra that not even the shaking of the whole mountain could affect in the slightest one who is perfectly liberated and enlightened.

II. 2. (*Sīho*). The opposition of Māra to the Buddha is seen to be stimulated on an occasion when he finds the Buddha teaching the Dhamma to the people. (See also suttas 4 (*Patirūpaṃ*) and 6 (*Pattaṃ*). His role as the opponent of the Buddha is emphasized: he announces himself as a 'challenging wrestler.' Once again he is represented as refusing to accept the Buddha's supremacy—or unable to believe it.

II. 5. (*Mānasaṃ*). Again Māra appears to believe that he can bind the Buddha with his 'snare'—namely, the wavering quality of the human mind, which he can usually turn to his own profit.

II. 6. (*Pattaṃ*) Māra's army (*Mārasenā*) is here mentioned the first and only time in the Māra Saṃyutta. Apart from this occasion, and that described in the Dhītaro Sutta (III. 5), where he appears with his three daughters, Māra always appears in the Māra Saṃyutta as a single, unaccompanied figure. There is danger from Māra's forces throughout the three realms, Kāmaloka, Rūpaloka and Arūpaloka (these are understood in the word *sabbaṭṭhānesu*); only those who have reached the transcendent realm of Nibbāna are safe from Māra. This idea is expressed again in the next sutta (II. 7). Here it is said that a follower of Buddha, he who possesses mindfulness, passing beyond the realm of Māra (*Māradheyya*), shines forth like the sun. Probably implied in these words is the idea that Māra's realm is one of darkness or obscurity.

II. 8. (*Piṇḍaṃ*) This sutta contains the noteworthy idea that even Māra acquires bad *karma* by his wicked actions, although he himself believes this is not so. This suggests that Māra is an office which is held successively by beings who are of appropriate evil *karma*. As a personal being Māra has no eternal existence.

II. 10 (*Rajjaṃ*) Māra appears here in the somewhat unusual role of the Buddha's apparent well-wisher. 'Let the Exalted One, Lord, exercise governance, let the Blessed One rule without smiting or causing others to smite, without conquering or causing others to conquer, without sorrowing or causing others sorrow, and therewithal ruling righteously.' The Buddha had been contemplating how difficult it was for kings to govern thus. The voice of Māra is immediately recognized by the Buddha, and hearing such advice from such a quarter he asks Māra what he has in view in speaking to him thus.

In reply Māra concedes the Buddha's great achievement in connexion with the four *iddhipādas*, or paths to miraculous power: he has developed them, practised them, made a 'vehicle' of them, established them, persevered and persisted in them, and applied them to good effect. Therefore, adds Māra, if the Buddha wishes he can turn the Himalaya into a mass of gold. The inference is that the Buddha possesses the power to provide himself with the means to establish himself as a king—and then rule righteously. Therefore, let him do so!

The Buddha points at once to the fallacy in the argument. The love of gold is treacherous; no man would ever remain satisfied for long, however much gold he received; it would be folly to proceed by such methods. 'This let us learn and shape our lives accordingly (*iti vidvā samañcare*). For when a man has seen whence sorrow arises, how shall he ever pay homage to sensual desires?'

This rejection of the misuse of the *iddhipāda* for ends which are only speciously good, and which are in fact illusory, is very striking. It contrasts with a good deal of contemporary religious practice on the one hand, and on the other it suggests some interesting parallels with the way that Satan in the New Testament is thought of as offering men that which is speciously good. Māra, like Satan, is regarded as operating in highly subtle ways.

III. 1. (*Sambahulā*). The bhikkhus, engaged in concentration, are approached by Māra in the guise of an old brahman. He urges them not to abandon too soon the pleasures of life—not to abandon that which is immediately present for the sake of that which comes in due time, later (*mā sandiṭṭhikaṃ hitvā kālikaṃ anudhāvittha*). They reply, in apparent agreement, but with an ingenious reversal of the sense of the words, that they have indeed abandoned what comes in due time (i.e. in the Buddhist understanding, the evil consequences of *taṇhā* etc.) for the sake of what can be enjoyed now (i.e. enlightenment). To this answer Māra can make no further reply, and retires beaten. When they recount the incident to the Buddha, he understands and tells them this was Māra, trying to 'darken their understanding'. It will be noted that although they were unaware of the presence of Māra, yet by their answer, faithful to Buddhist doctrine, they successfully overcame him.

III. 2. (*Samiddhi*). Māra's presence is manifested by a loud and terrible noise. To non-Buddhists this would have meant the presence of some hostile yakkha. It will be noted that although Samiddhi was engaged in meditation, Māra still made his presence felt. The bhikkhu is thus not immune from Māra's attacks, even when meditating, but he is able not to be overcome by them.

III. 3 (*Godhika*) Māra's opposition to Godhika's decease, as an Arahat, is strongly emphasized; it is also entirely unavailing, so puny is Māra's power beside that of the Arahat's. The Evil One is conceived here in picturesque fashion as 'a smokiness, a murkiness'; the 'dark' aspect of Māra's nature is again emphasized. Māra's very limited knowledge is also demonstrated; he seeks in the four directions of the compass for what he cannot possibly find—the consciousness (*viññāṇa*) of Godhika. This was beyond Māra's ability to find because Godhika, as the Buddha explained to the bhikkhus, had become *parinibbuta*, that is, he had entered Nibbāna, which transcends spatial conceptions. Godhika is said to have conquered Māra's forces because he had freed himself of craving and its root, namely, ignorance. It will be noted that the closing line refers to Māra as a *yakkha*: *tato so dummano yakkho tath'ev'-antaradhāyatha*.

III. 4. (*Sattavassāni*) The seven years here referred to, during which Māra has been pursuing the Buddha, are explained by the Pali commentary as 'six years before the Enlightenment and one after.' That is to say, during the six years of the austerities and during one year now of the Buddhahood. All this time Māra has been waiting for an opportunity to 'come down on him' (*otārāpekkho*), and has found none.

Māra reproaches the Buddha for his life of lonely meditation. The Buddha's reply emphasizes that since the root of sorrow has been eradicated from his life he can meditate free from guilt and with mind free from all sorrow. For he is *anāsavo*, that is, freed from the *āsavas*, (the 'influx' or intoxications of *moha*). This contrasts with the epithet here applied to Māra by the Buddha—*pamattabandhu*, that is, kin to all those who *are* intoxicated (i.e. by *moha*).

The sutta concludes with the simile of the crab, pulled out of the water, and with claws broken and smashed, unable to return; this, declares Māra, is what has happened to him, in his encounters with the Buddha, all his wiles and stratagems have been shattered, and he is utterly powerless where the Buddha is concerned.

There follow the *gāthā* which appear also in the Padhāna Sutta (Sn 447, 448), in which Māra compares himself with a crow that circles a stone, thinking it was something good to eat; as that crow pecked at what proved to be a rock, so also Māra disgusted takes his leave of the Buddha.

Having spoken these verses, Māra is said to sit down near by, disconsolately scratching at the earth with a stick. The whole effect is cumulative; picturesque similes are piled up, and the image of a broken, disappointed and dejected Māra is powerfully conveyed to even the simplest intellect.

III. 5. (*Dhītaro*)

As it stands this forms an apparent continuation of the previous sutta, and, like the Sattavassāni, it departs from the usual form of the Māra suttas.

Māra is approached by his three daughters, Taṇhā, Arati and Ragā [*sic*], upon which he discloses to them the reason for his dejection: 'It is not easy to capture the Arahat, the Blessed One of the earth, by means of passion, for he transcends Māra's realm; this is why I am full of sorrow.'

Thereupon Māra's three daughters approach the Buddha, and seek to distract him by assuming the shapes of a variety of women of all ages. When this proves useless they admit to each other the truth of what Māra had said regarding the

Buddha. Any other samaṇa or brahman would have been overcome by now. A further approach to the Buddha is then made, and Taṇhā speaks a verse, identical with that spoken by Māra at the beginning of the Sattavassāni Sutta, asking him why he meditates thus alone, and whether he has no friends. The Buddha's reply is different here from his reply when Māra spoke these words, and is made appropriate to the circumstances: 'Now that the host of sweet and pleasant shapes has been repulsed, I'm seated here alone, and meditate upon the good I've won. . . .' He emphasizes his solitariness, and that he has need of no one's company.

Arati also then addresses him, and questions whether, although 'the five floods' have been crossed it is possible for him to cross the sixth—whether it is possible for one who is continually meditating to escape lustful *thought* (kāmasaññā). Again, the Buddha's reply shows the futility of the attempt to assail him 'whose body is tranquil and whose mind is fully liberated (*passadhakāyo suvimuttacitto*), who produces no new volitions (*asaṇkhārāno*) who is contemplative and homeless (*satimā anoko*), who knows the Dhamma (*aññāya dhammaṃ*), and who meditates free from mental restlessness (*avitakkajhāyī*), and had no anger, no memories, no clogging of the mind (*na kuppati na sarati ve na thīno*). This reply indicates the earlier, pre-monastic ideal of the homeless solitary recluse, and suggests that such a way of life was conceived to be the prime condition for overcoming all the subtle assaults of the Lord of this world.

When it is Ragā's turn to speak the case is apparently regarded as hopeless and she can only lament that this homeless man (*anoko*, repeated) will deny the Death-King (*maccurājā*) of many subjects.

The three daughters finally return to Māra, and receive a suitably abusive tirade upon the foolishness of their attempt.

These last two suttas, coming as they do at the end of a collection which describes the persistent and subtle efforts of Māra to assail the Buddha, have the effect of demonstrating the utter ineffectiveness of Māra wherever the Buddha is concerned, and thus, of emphasizing the deliverance from Māra which is ensured for those who follow the Buddha's way.

The Bhikkhunī Saṃyutta. This comprises ten suttas of fairly uniform character, each consisting of (a) a conventional introduction; (b) words spoken to the bhikkhunī by Māra; (c) the recognition of Māra by the bhikkhunī (again, in a set form); (d) a verse spoken by the bhikkhunī; and (e) a conventional ending.

(a) The narrative introduction in each case describes the bhikkhunī's retirement to some solitary place, at the foot of a tree (the recognized place for meditation). This immediately provokes Māra, who approaches with the intention of arousing fear, wavering of mind, and dread; this is the conventional form of words throughout the four suttas (*bhayaṃ chambhitattaṃ lomahaṃsaṃ uppādetu- kāmo*); and desirous also of making her desist from being alone, or from meditation (*vivekamhā cāvetu-kāmo*; *samādhimhā cāvetu-kāmo*).

(b) The method by which Māra seeks to achieve this is not, as in some other cases, by making terrifying sounds, but by addressing the bhikkhunī concerned with a suggestion, or a rebuke, or with contempt, or argumentatively. Thus to Āḷavikā: 'Never shall you find escape while in the world! What profits then this loneliness?'; to Somā: 'What sages attain is very hard to win! What may a woman hope to achieve. . . . ?'; to Gotamī: 'Why are you sitting alone, so tearful? Is it a man you are seeking?'; to Vijayā he pretends to be a youthful lover; to the beautiful Uppalavaṇṇā. he speaks of the dangers that threaten her from possible seducers; to Cālā, Upacālā and Sīsupacālā he addresses questions intended to lead them astray, concerning rebirth and other 'ensnaring' subjects; Selā and Vajirā he tries to engage in speculations (*diṭṭhi*): 'Who was it made the human puppet's form?'; 'Whence does a being (*satta*) arise, and where does a being cease and pass away?'

(c) In every case the bhikkhunī's response is: 'Who now is this, human or non-human, who speaks. . . . ? Surely it is Marā the Evil One!' The possibility of the words having been spoken by a human voice would serve to remind the hearers of the sutta that a human voice may in fact sometimes be the voice of Māra: Māra's suggestions may come through the words of other people. In this way, just as much as by means of terrifying sights or noises, it is inferred, Māra seeks to frighten the disciple from the path, or draw him aside with doubts.

(d) The reply made by the bhikkhunī is sometimes addressed directly to Māra (as in suttas Nos. 1–5, and 10), and sometimes it takes the form simply of an affirmation of faith in the Dhamma, revealed by the Buddha and confirmed in experience (*atthi nissaraṇam loke paññāya me suphussitaṃ*) (sutta 1), and sometimes includes a rejection of all sense-pleasures, or, in the case of attempts to involve them in speculations, a rejection of all speculative opinions (*Māradiṭṭhigatam nu te*) (sutta 10). The last two suttas, particularly, manifest an outlook which is in principle, and in some of the terminology used, that of the Abhidhamma literature. The last gātha, spoken by Vajirā, is in fact quoted in the fifth book of the Abhidhamma-piṭaka, the Kathāvatthu, as well as in the Milinda-pañha (i. 45) and the Visuddhimagga (ch. xviii).

(e) The suttas end, in every case, with the lament by Māra that he has been 'recognized'—which is always Māra's undoing —(*jānāti maṃ. . . . bhikkhunī*), and his consequent sorrowful departure from the scene (*dukkhī dummano tath' ev' antar-adhāyīti*).

Apart from the *Mārasaṃyutta* and the *Bhikkhunīsaṃyutta* there are in the Saṃyutta Nikaya three further references to Māra of a legendary nature.

There is the Mahāparinibbāna narrative, here found at S V. 258 ff.; this does not depart in any significant way from the account already examined.

Secondly there is a brief reference in Sutta 10 of the Nānātitthiya Vagga. (S I. 65 f.) The Buddha, staying near Rājagaha, is visited by various devaputtas, who, addressing the Buddha in turn, speak the praise of various notable teachers who ranked among the rivals of the Buddha; these praises are summed up in the words of Ākoṭaka:

> 'Distinguished friars, each of a school the leader,
> From saintly men these are in sooth not distant.'
> (C. A. F. Rhys Davids translation—p. 91).

This statement is refuted by the devaputta named Veṭambari, who declares that none of these ascetics is worthy even of comparison with the Buddha. At this point Māra speaks, standing beside Veṭambari, making it seem as though the words were the latter's (he took his shape, says the commentary, making the devaputta appear to contradict himself). Māra's words praise the austerities of the ascetic-teachers, and conclude with the affirmation that these men, bound as they are for another world, do indeed give good advice to men. To the

Buddha it is clear who has really spoken these words, and he addressed the Evil One in a verse. Māra's praises, he says, are always like a bait, cast for the purpose of catching and destroying the prey (*āmisaṃ va macchānaṃ vadhāya khitta*).

Thirdly, there is the story of the suicide of Vakkali (S III. 123 f.) which appears to be a doublet of the latter part of the story of Godhika, already encountered in the Mārasaṃyutta. So far as the Māra legend is concerned it does not appear to offer any material not found in the story of Godhika.

(III) *Didactic references*

The references to Māra which are of a didactic nature are in this Nikāya fairly numerous, and in some cases they are of particular interest, while for the rest they help to confirm what has already been noted concerning Māra.

In the Nidāna Vagga, Māra is described as a fisherman whose hook, 'flesh-baited' (*āmisagata*) is swallowed by those fish which have 'an eye to flesh' (*āmisacakkhumaccho*), and who thus fall into misfortune or disaster (S II. 226). In the following sutta Māra is said to be like a hunter who, with corded harpoon, shoots a tortoise swimming in a forbidden pool, so that the tortoise is utterly unable to escape (S II. 227). The details of this parable seem to be arranged to fit in with preconceived ideas about Māra; the forbidden pool, for example, corresponds with the 'pastures not his own', where walking the bhikkhu is said to be in danger from Māra (D III. 58 for example). Māra's harpoon, like his hook in the previous sutta, is explained in the text as meaning gains, favour and flattery (*lābhasakkārasiloko*); while the cord by which the victim is held fast, unable to escape, is lustful enjoyment (*nandirāga*). This idea, that Māra traps men by those things which are superficially attractive reveals a conception of Māra which is similar in this respect to that of Satan, the deceiver.

Māra is said to have no access to bhikkhus who sleep on beds of straw: 'strenuous are they, and ardent in their energy' (*appamattā ātāpino upāsanasmiṃ*—S. II 268), but bhikkhus who sleep on soft couches are open to Māra's access, and against them he will find occasion for profiting (*lacchati otāram . . . ārammaṇam*). What is emphasized here is not so much the deceptive nature of Māra, as the seemingly innocuous paths that may lead men to fall into Māra's power: one must be constantly on the alert, and whatever results in relaxation of vigilance and ardour is playing into Māra's hands.

The reminder that Māra is conquered through ardent meditation is repeated in sutta 4 of the Bhikkhu-saṃyutta (S II. 277 ff.). The Buddha, referring to one who is said to be able to attain the four *jhānas* at will, says that such a bhikkhu bears the final body, he has conquered Māra and his mount (*dhāreti antimaṃ dehaṃ jetvā Māraṃ savāhanaṃ*—S II. 278). Precisely the same words occur in the next sutta, where they are used to describe Sujāta, another bhikkhu of whom it is said that he is able to enter at will into the highest state of meditation (S II. 279); he too conquers Māra. The same is said in sutta 12 of two other bhikkhus; (S II. 285) The tendency described as grasping or clinging (*upādiyamāno*) is said by the Buddha to constitute being bound by Māra, whereas he in whom no such grasping is found is said to be released from Māra (*upādiyamāno kho bhikkhu baddho Mārassa anupādiyamāno mutto pāpimato* S III. 73). The bhikkhu to whom these words are addressed is asked if he understands what is meant by this. He replies that if one clings to that which is of bodily form, he is Māra's bondsman (*rūpaṃ kho bhante upādiyamāno baddho Mārassa*); this statement is then repeated similarly for each of the other four skandhas (*vedanaṃ kho. . . . saññaṃ kho. . . . saṅkhāre kho. . . . viññāṇaṃ kho. . . .*). In the same manner the activity described as imagining (*maññamāno*) is said to constitute bondage to Māra, and the whole of the previous explanation of upādiymāno is repeated with reference to maññamāno. And similarly again for the activity described as 'being enamoured' (*abhinandamāno*) (S III. 74 f.). In all these respects one may be bound by Māra.

In the Rādha-Saṃyutta (III. 188 ff.) there are further long sections devoted to Māra. These are given in reply to the question which Rādha asks the Buddha: 'They say, Māra! Māra! How far is there a Māra?' The question itself raises a point of interest for it would appear to reflect either (a) a non-Buddhist popular habit of using the name Māra; or, (b) the extent to which the Buddha's special teaching about Māra had been disseminated at the time this sutta was composed.

There is very little evidence to support the first of these alternatives; it seems more likely that 'they say' refers to the currency of the term Māra among those most deeply influenced by the Buddha's doctrine. The asking of the question suggests that the conception of Māra, associated with the Buddha, was nevertheless, even then, imperfectly understood. The term was apparently being used without a full appreciation of its significance in connection with Buddhist teaching; it needed to be clarified, and it is the purpose of this sutta to do so.

The answer given is that where there is corporeality (*rūpa*) there is Māra, or that which is of the nature of Māra—literally that which kills, the destroyer (*Māretā*), or that which is passing away or dying (*yo mīyati*) (*Rūpe kho Rādha sati Māro vā assa māretā vā yo vā pana mīyati*—S III. 189). With regard to whatever is corporeal, therefore, Rādha is exhorted to regard it as of the nature of Māra, as perishing, as pain, as a source of pain.

This answer to the question is then repeated four times; what has been said of rūpa is applied successively to feeling (*vedanā*), perception (*saññā*), mental formations (*saṇkhāra*) and consciousness (*viññāṇa*).

Thus each of the five khandhas is to be regarded as of the nature of Māra; that is to say, all the factors or elements of sensory existence are regarded as nothing more or less than Māra, and they who regard existence in this way regard it rightly, it is said (*ye nam evam passanti te sammāpassantī ti*—S III. 189). This way of regarding the khandhas is intended to arouse disgust, which in turn will bring about dispassion; dispassion is to bring about release, and release means Nibbāna, the goal of the holy life (S III. 189). In this way the Buddha uses Rādha's question about Māra as a means of directing his attention to Nibbāna.

The question about Māra (who he is), with the same answer, identifying him with the five khandhas, and urging aversion from them and thus release, is repeated in two further suttas of the Rādha-saṃyutta, Nos. 11 and 12 (S III. 195). In suttas 23, 24, 35 and 36 it is said that desire (*chanda*) and lust (*rāga*) for whatever is "Māra" must be put away (S III. 198 and 200).

The question about Māra occurs again in a slightly different form in the Saḷāyatana-saṃyutta (S IV. 38 f.). Here it is Samiddhi who asks: '*Māro Māroti vuccati; kittāvatā nu kho bhante Māro vā assa Mārapaññatti vā ti.*' (Mārapaññatti, the 'symptoms of Māra', the commentary explains as Māra's realm). The answer to the question is also slightly different here from that given before; Māra is explained as being not, in this case, the five khandhas, but the six faculties (eye, ear, nose, tongue, body and mind), the six objective elements (*rūpa, sota* etc.), the six kinds of consciousness (*cakkhuviññāṇa* etc.), and the six kinds of things cognizable in these various ways (*cakkhuviññāṇaviññātabbā dhammā* etc.). This is yet another of the schemes by which Buddhism analyses the whole of sensory existence. But in both answers to the question there is the common feature, that Māra is equated with the totality of sensory existence, however analysed. It will be evident that this conception of Māra is considerably removed from that of Māra as a yakkha; the fact that he is conceived in both these ways, animistic and abstract, constitutes the significance of the Māra symbol.

A variation of the kind of teaching about Māra that has just been noted is to be found in the Saḷāyatana-saṃyutta, in the sutta entitled 'The Tortoise'. Here the teaching is in the form of a parable about a jackal watching a tortoise which has its five extremities withdrawn into its shell, waiting for one of them to be thrust forth, so that he can seize it, and thus master the tortoise. So, it is said, Māra waits at the five doors of the human faculties, unceasingly on the watch for a chance to seize his victim. 'Wherefore, brethren, abide keeping watch over the doors of the faculties. So long as you abide keeping watch over the door of the faculties, Māra the Evil One will go away in disgust, not getting an opportunity' (S IV. 178). The same idea is found again, this time in the teaching of Moggallāna, in the sutta entitled *Avassuto* (S IV. 185, 186). Whoever abides lustful after objects cognizable by the eye (ear, nose, tongue, touch and mind) is as exposed to Māra's attack as a roof of dry thatch is vulnerable to fire. But one who abides not lustful after objects of the senses is as immune to Māra's attacks as a house built of clay and plaster is immune to fire.

Māra's bondage is the theme of certain other passages. The 'Chapter on the Worldly Sensual Elements' (*Lokakāmuguṇa-vagga*, S IV. 91 ff.) begins with a sutta entitled *Māra-pāsa*. One who delights in objects cognizable by the eye, and welcomes them, and clings to them, is said to have 'gone under Māra's sway', 'Māra's noose encircles him, bound is he with Māra's bond. And conversely, one who does not delight in these things, is not under Māra's sway, unwound for him is Māra's noose, freed is he from Māra's bond, (S IV. 91). In another passage Māra's subjects are said to be those whom longing for rebirth destroys, those who simply drift down the stream of becoming, that is, who make no effort to be released (S IV. 128). The analogy of the fisherman occurs again, in the sutta entitled Bālisiko (S IV. 158). Like the baited hook cast by the fisherman are the six 'hooks' on which the unwary are caught and come to destruction, namely the five kinds of objects perceived by the senses, together with objects perceived by the mind (S IV. 159). The extreme subtlety of Māra's bondage is described in the Yavakalāpi sutta (S IV. 202). It is even more subtle than that bondage which bound Vepacitti, lord of the asuras, when he was prisoner of the devas. Whoever holds to a dogma, he is Māra's bondsman: *maññamāno kho bhikkhave baddho Mārassa*. Examples of dogma are then provided; to say, 'I am', 'This I am' etc., these are the kind of dogmas that must be renounced.

In sutta 43 of the Bojjhaṇga-Saṃyutta (S V. 99) the way for crushing Māra's host is described (*Mārasenapamaddanam . . . maggam*). This consists of the seven factors of enlightenment (*satta bojjhaṇgā*). The seven are: mindfulness (*sati*), investigation of the Dhamma (*dhammavicaya*), energy (*viriya*), rapture (*pīti*), tranquility (*passaddhi*), concentration (*samādhi*), and equanimity (*upekkhā*).

In suttas 6 and 7 of the Satipaṭṭhāna-Saṃyutta are found respectively the parable of the Falcon (S V. 146 f.), and of the Monkey (S V. 148 f.). Both of these stories are made to illustrate the teaching that Māra obtains access to any who roam outside their proper range (*Agocare caratam paravisaye lacchati Māro otāraṃ lacchati Māro ārammaṇaṃ*). That which is not one's proper range but Māra's, is the realm of the five sensual elements (*pañca kāmaguṇa*). These are then elaborated; they consist of objects cognizable by the eye (*cakkhuviññeyyā rūpā*), sounds cognizable by the ear (*sotaviññeyyā saddā*), and similarly for the nose, the tongue, and the touch (*ghānaviññeyyā gandhā, jivhāviññeyyā rasā, kāyaviññeyyā phoṭṭhabbā*). All this, it is emphasized, is Māra's range. The statement is then made in its reverse form, that those who keep to their own range are not accessible to Māra (*gocare carataṃ sake pettike visaye na lacchati Māro ārammanaṃ*). The bhikkhu's proper range is then explained as the realm of the four Applications of Mindfulness (*cattāro satipaṭṭhānā*). These are set out at length; they are described also in the Satipaṭṭhāna-Suttas of the Dīgha- and Majjhima-Nikāyas (D 22; M 10), where the description of them is both prefaced and followed by the words, 'The only way that leads to the attainment of purity, to the overcoming of sorrow and lamentation, to the end of pain and grief, to the entering of the right path, and the realization of Nibbāna, are the four Applications of Mindfulness' (D II. 290; M I. 55 f.).

5 KHUDDAKA NIKĀYA

(a) *Dhammapada*

The passages in the Dhammapada in which allusion is made to Māra come within the category of didactic material. There are fourteen of these, and they are fairly evenly spaced throughout the book.

The first to be considered is a passage where it said that certain things predispose a person to being overthrown by Māra: namely, to live contemplating pleasant things, to have the senses unrestrained (*asaṃvuta*), to be immoderate in eating, slothful, of low (spiritual) vigour (*hīnavīriya*) (Dh 7). By contrast, the next verse speaks of the things which prevent a person from being overthrown by Māra: to contemplate the unpleasant aspects of life, to keep the senses well restrained, to be temperate in eating, to have trustful confidence (*saddha*), and to be resolute in (spiritual) vigour (*āraddhavīriya*) (Dh 8).

It is noteworthy that the order is: moral strength (or weakness); then, depending upon that condition, either victory over Māra or defeat by Māra. The condition or attitude of the person concerned is the primary element; Māra's success or failure follows as a consequence.

It is also clear from the Dhammapada that the conditions of human life are such that men in general are likely to be easily assailable by Māra. This is expressed in the words of verse 34: just as a fish flung upon dry land twitches and writhes, so normally does human consciousness (*citta*). This constant 'fluttering' of the mind constitutes a great danger, and its mention leads here to the exhortation to beware of (i.e. to shun) the realm of Māra (*pariphandati 'dam cittam, māradheyyam pahātave*—Dh 34). (Here, *pahātave* is understood as equivalent to *pahātabba*, as Nārada Thera points out in the notes to his translation[1]). Another approach to this idea is found in verse 37, where it is said that those who bring the mind under control are free from the fetter of Māra: *ye cittam saññamessanti*

[1] *The Dhammapada*, Wisdom of the East Series (London, 1954).

mokkhanti mārabandhanā. Once again the order is to be seen: the disciple's effort (or the absence of it); Māra is defeated (or is the victor).

Māra should be fought by means of the weapon of *wisdom*; this is the teaching contained in verse 40, and the 'wisdom' there referred to consists of realizing that the body is only as endurable as an earthenware pot, and of having the consciousness guarded like a fortress:

> *Kumbhūpamaṃ kāyam imaṃ viditvā*
> *nagarūpamaṃ cittam idam ṭhapetvā*
> *yodhetha māraṃ paññāvudhena*
> *jitaṃ ca rakkhe anivesano siyā.*

Māra's inheritance of the role of Kāma, as well as that of Mṛtyu, is well illustrated in verse 46. He who realizes that the body is only as endurable as foam is described as breaking off the flower-tipped darts of Māra:

> *phenūpamaṃ kāyam imaṃ viditvā ...*
> *chetvāna mārassa papupphakāni*
> *adassanaṃ maccurājassa gacche* (cf. Dh 7).

The 'flower-tipped dart' is a feature of the mythology of Kāma, as Radhakrishnan points out in the notes to his translation, where he recalls such examples as *puṣpabāna, kusumāyudha.* He who is impervious to these flower-tipped darts (that is, the danger that lurks in what is superficially attractive), evades King Death (Maccurājā). Here, as in the Itivuttaka, Maccu is clearly an alternative name for Māra, who has already been mentioned in this verse.

The association of Māra with death and rebirth is implied again in verse 337. The hearer is exhorted to dig out the root of craving, so that Māra may not break him again and again (in death after death), as the river-flood season after season destroys the reeds at its bank.

> *taṇhāya mūlam khaṇatha usīrattho va bīraṇam*
> *mā vo naḷaṃva soto va māro bhañji punappunam* (cf. Dh 48).

In all the other verses which contain references to Māra, the theme may be said to be the conquering or deluding of Māra.

In verse 57 it is said that Māra never gets on to the trail of those who are rich by virtue, who live careful lives, and who are liberated by right insight (*tesaṃ. . . . Māro maggam na vindati.* (cf. Dh 8).

In v. 105 it is said that no deva or gandhabba, not ever Māra together with Brahmā can reverse the victory which has been gained by the man who has conquered self (described in the previous verse, 104, *attā have jitam*).

Maccurājā is mentioned again in v. 170, in a context closely similar to that already noted in v. 46.

It is the *dhīrā* who overcome Māra and his hosts (v. 175). These, the 'inspired ones' or the 'wise', travel beyond the world (*nīyanti dhīrā lokamhā*), and have overcome Māra and his army (*vāhiṇī*), or, in the alternative reading, Māra and his mount (*vāhanaṃ*).

The deluding or bewildering of Māra is referred to in v. 274, where it is said to be result of a man's walking in the holy eightfold way: *etamhi tumhe paṭipajjatha, mārass' etaṃ pamohanam.*

The word *pamohana* (which is here preferred by the *PED* and others[1] to the reading *pamocana*) is explained in the Dhammapada commentary by *vañcana*. The idea is evidently that of deluding or even deceiving Māra; by inference this draws attention to an idea which is not uncommon in the Suttas, namely, Māra's limited knowledge or range of vision,

The necessity for exercising energy in following the Buddhist path is emphasized in v. 276: 'You yourself must strive. The Blessed Ones are (only) preachers. Those who enter the path and practise meditation are released from the bondage of Māra.' (Radhakrishnan's translation). This last sentence provides a clear and succinct summary of the teaching given throughout this book, on the subject of Māra: *paṭipannā pamokkhanti jhāyino mārabandhanā.*

Finally, in verse 350, it may be noted, the same idea is found again:

vittakūpasame ca yo rato
asubhaṃ bhāvayatī sadā sato
esa kho vyantikāhiti
esacchecchati mārabandhanaṁ (Dh 350).

It is a point of some significance that in the previous verse (349) *bandhana* is mentioned, but without any allusion to Māra, and this apparently without any loss of force in the words. The

[1] Radhakrishnan, and Nārada Thera, in their translations.

fetter may be understood as that which holds the man whose craving grows and grows: *taṇhā pavaddhati esa kho daḷhaṃ karoti bandhanaṃ* (Dh 349). It will be seen from this that the reference to Māra in v. 350, in connexion with *bandhana*, might there also have been omitted, without the sense as a whole being affected. In other words, what these two verses taken together illustrate is the way in which the teaching moves between mythological and abstract metaphysical forms of expression. In this sense, these two verses are representative of the Dhammapada as a whole: the Māra references are not of central importance, and abstract terms are more often used to convey the ideas which the Māra image conveys. Nevertheless the Māra references remain; and it would be difficult to give an exposition of the Dhammapada without giving an account of who Māra was.

(b) *Udāna*

(i) *Formulas.* One instance of the conventional formula, with its mention of Māra, is found in this short work. This occurs in the words of the Buddha in sutta 5 of the Pāṭaligāmiya Vagga (Ud 82), and is an example of a kind already noted: *nāhan tañ Cunda passāmi sadevake loke samārake sabrahmake sassamaṇabrāhmaṇiyā pajāya sadevamānussāya. . . .*

(ii) *Legendary material.* The Māra material under this heading in the Udānaṃ is found in the Mahāparinibbāna-Sutta. Ananda's possession by Māra is recorded. Māra's approach to the Buddha, urging him to enter *parinibbāna*, and the Buddha's reply to Māra exactly as in the Dīgha Nikāya. The reason for its inclusion here in the Udānaṃ is evidently, as Windisch notes (*op. cit.*, p. 35), the occurrence of *Udānaṃ* among the words which introduce the verse with which the quotation of the Mahāparinibbāna Sutta in this book ends: *atha kho bhagavā etam atthaṃ viditvā tāyaṃ velāyaṃ imaṃ udānaṃ udānesi* . . . (Ud 64).

(iii) *Didactic material.* 1. The association of Māra with darkness is attested in the words of the Buddha found in sutta 3 of the Bodhi-Vagga:

> *yadā have pātubhavanti dhammā ātāpino jhāyato brahmaṇassa vidhūpayaṃ tiṭṭhati Mārasenaṃ sūriyo'va obhāsayam antalikkhan ti* (Ud 3).

Māra's hosts are routed by the ardent, meditating saint, as the darkness by the sun. If things become plain, or appear clearly (pātubhavanti), when Māra's hosts are routed, it is evident that Māra is to be thought of as making things obscure, or confused.

2. The close connexion of Māra with the round of rebirth is implied in two suttas of the Udānaṃ. Su. 10 of the Nanda Vagga concludes with a verse which has as its final lines:

tassa nibbutassa bhikkhuno anupādā punabhavo no hoti
abhibhūto Māro vijitasangāmo, upaccagā sabbabhavāni
tādī ti. (Ud 33).

Thus, he who is *nibbuta*, he who is free from renewed existence (*punabhava*), of him it is said: Māra is beaten (*abhibhūto Māro*).

Similarly in sutta 10 of the Maghiya-Vagga, it is said of the bhikkhu whose mind is calmed, and who has cut the cord of rebirth, that he is freed from Māra's bondage: *mutto so Māra-bandhanā* (Ud. 46).

3. In sutta 2 of the Meghiya-Vagga it is said of him whose life is unguarded (*arakkhitena kāyena*), and who is given to false views (*micchādiṭṭhigatena*), that he is delivered into Māra's power (*vasaṃ Mārassa gacchati*) (Ud 38). Such were the bhikkhus who are described in this sutta; they were 'frivolous, empty-handed, busy-bodies, of harsh speech, loose in talk, lacking concentration, unsteady, not composed, of flighty mind, with senses uncontrolled.'[1] It will be seen from this description of some typical victims of Māra that the Evil One's power manifests itself in human life not necessarily in any marked degree of viciousness, but at a very ordinary level of careless behaviour and speech.

4. The contrast with such behaviour is seen in sutta 10 of the Sonatherassa-Vagga; the bhikkhu in whom mindfulness is established, is said to attain excellence (he wins calm followed by insight, says the commentary), and thus passes beyond Māra's range of vision: *adassanam Maccurājassa gacche ti* (Ud 61). Here it will be noted, the name *Maccu* is used; from the sense of this and other passages of a similar nature where Māra is mentioned in the same terms, it is evident that Maccu is being used as an alternative name for Māra.

[1] F. L. Woodward, *Minor Anthologies of the Pāli Canon Part II*. p. 45.

(c) *Itivuttaka*

(i) *Formulas.* In two passages in the Itivuttaka the conventional cosmic formula which contains the name Māra occurs.

In sutta 4 of Vagga III faith is praised 'which cannot be uprooted by anyone in the world: '*saddhā. . . . asaṃhāriyā samaṇena vā brahmaṇena vā devena vā mārena vā brahmunā vā kenaci vā lokasmiṃ*—(It 77).

In sutta 13 of Vagga IV, whatever exists in the whole world, it is said, is fully comprehended by the Tathāgata: '*yaṃ bhikkhave sadevakassa lokassa samārakassa sabrahmakassa sassamaṇabrāhmaṇiyā pajāya sadevamanussāya. . . . tam tathāgatena abhisambuddhaṃ*'—It 121. It is, among other reasons, on account of this ability fully to comprehend the whole world of beings that he is called Tathāgata (*tasmā tathāgato ti vuccati*—It 121). This statement is repeated, both in the sutta, and in the verse which follows; it is because he comprehends the whole world that he is free from it (*sabbalokam abhiññāya. . . . sabbalokavisaṃyutto*).

Once again Māra appears as an element of the world, as it is *supernaturally* seen and known by the Enlightened One.

(ii) There are no references in the Itivuttaka which belong to the category of the Māra-legends.

(iii) *Didactic material.* References to Māra which are of a didactic nature make up most of the list of passages to be considered in the Itivuttaka (9 out of 14). The following doubtful readings will not be taken into consideration: the occurrence of the name Māra in the verses in sutta 38 of Vagga II, where two Burmese MSS. have *māram*, but three others have *mānam*, and two others *mājaham*; and similarly in the first verse of sutta 9 of Vagga II. However, in the second of the verses attached to this sutta there is a clear reference:

> *Tasmā sadā jhānaratā samāhitā*
> *ātāpino jātikhayantadassino*
> *māraṃ sasenaṃ abhibhuyya bhikkhavo*
> *bhavatha jātimaraṇassa pāragā ti* (It 40).

Here again Māra is connected with rebirth; those who overcome him and his hosts transcend birth and death. The verse provides a further reminder that the overcoming of Māra is for those who 'delight in meditation' (*jhānaratā*), whose mind is composed (*samāhitā*), and who are 'ardent' (*ātāpino*).

The connexion of Māra with rebirth is emphasized again in sutta 8 of Vagga III, in words identical with those found in the Saṃyutta-Nikāya (S II. 278); he who has freed himself from the three āsavas (*kāmā, bhavā* and *avijjā*) bears his last body, having conquered Māra and his mount (*dhāreti antimaṃ dehaṃ jetvā māraṃ savāhanaṃ*—It 50). It is worthy of notice that it is the threefold list of the *Āsavas* which is found here; this is probably older than the fourfold form (which includes *diṭṭhi* also). This suggests that this verse concerning Māra comes from earlier rather than later material.

Māra and rebirth are found associated again in the following sutta (vagga III. 9). Here the opposite case, of those who are still in bondage to Māra, is mentioned. They are described also as those still bound with the fetter of craving (*taṇhā*):

> *taṇhāyogena saṃyuttā rattacittā bhavābhave*
> *te yogayuttā mārassa ayogakkhemino janā*
> *sattā gacchanti saṃsāraṃ jātimaraṇagāmino.* (It 50).

Thus the two descriptions stand in parallel: *taṇhāyoga* and *yogayutta mārassa*; possibly the second is the more comprehensive of the two terms and is thought of as embracing the former; what is of special interest is that a metaphysical and a mythological expression for the same condition are found side by side in the one sentence. All who are thus fettered by *taṇhā/Māra*, continue in the round of birth and death.

The next sutta (III. 10—It 50 f.) deals with the three things, possessing which, the bhikkhu passes beyond Māra's realm and shines forth like the sun. These are: *sīla, samādhi* and *paññā*. This trio of terms constitute a well-known summary form of the holy eightfold path. He who is possessed of the qualities enumerated in the eightfold path is thus said to transcend Māra's realm (*Māradheyya*).

The idea that he who has transcended Māra's realm shines forth like the sun (*ādicco va virocati*) has already been encountered in the *Mārasaṃyutta* (II. 7) with its suggestion that Māra's realm is one of darkness or obscurity.

The line *dhāreti antimaṃ dehaṃ, jetvā Māraṃ savāhanaṃ*, already noted at III, 1. 8, occurs again at the end of the verse found in sutta 13 of Vagga III. Here it is applied to him who is: *indriyasampanno santo santipade rato* (It 53).

The connexion of Māra with rebirth finds expression again in sutta 20 of Vagga III (It 58). More precisely it is the connexion of *Maccurājā* with rebirth that is implied. Of him who is *apunabbhavāya* it is also said that *amohayi maccurājaṃ* and that he is *maccujaha*, he has left death behind.

The use of the name Māra in a passage where it provides a mythological parallel to the philosophical term *taṇhā* has already been noted (It 50). A similar example occurs in sutta 19 of Vagga III, where passion (*rāga*), hate (*dosa*) and delusion (*moha*) are spoken of as characteristics of Māra's bondage. By whom the three have not been abandoned, it is said, he is Māra's bondsman, Māra's noose encircles him, he is at the mercy of the Evil One (*bandho Mārassa paṭimukkassa mārapāso yathākāmakaranīyo ca pāpimato*—It 56). These three *mūlā* are connected with Māra's bondage in another passage, in connexion with the asuras (It 92). Renewed existence as an asura is one of four bad destinies (*dugg ati*, or *apāya*) which await those who are ignorant (*ajānantā*) of the three fires: *rāgaggi, dosaggi, mohaggi*. Of such it is said that they are *amuttā Mārabandhanā*.

The last of the passages from the Itivuttaka to be mentioned is one in which the life of the bhikkhu is equated with battling with Māra. (Tikanipāta vagga IV, sutta 3) (It 75). It is said that when a disciple goes forth from home to homelessness, then from the devas the cry is heard; Behold a holy disciple is thinking about battling with Māra! (*Eso ariyasāvako mārena saddhim sangāmāya ceteti*). Then, when the disciple abides in a state of absorption, the cry arises from the devas: *Eso ariyasāvako mārena saddhim sangāmeti!* Finally, when he has obtained release by insight he is acclaimed as having conquered in battle. Although it is not explicitly said that he has conquered Māra, this is obviously implied in the previous words of the devas. Thus, the life of meditation of the Buddhist ariyasāvako, is, mythologically, a life in which he is fighting and conquering Māra. (It 75).

(d) *Sutta Nipāta*

(i) *Conventional formulas.* These occur in three places.

1. In conversation with the brahman farmer Bhāradvāja the

Buddha says: *Na kho 'han taṃ brāhmaṇa passāmi sadevake loke samārake sabrahmake sassamaṇabrāhmaṇiyā pajāya sadeva-manussāya*. . . . Sn p. 15.

2. In the Sela Sutta the Buddha's fame is described; among other epithets applied to the Buddha here is 'world-knower' (*lokavidū*) (Sn p. 103). Three lines farther on this description is expanded into the sentence *so imaṃ lokaṃ sadevakaṃ samār-akaṃ sabrahmakaṃ*. . . . etc. . . . *abhiññā sacchikatvā pavedeti*. The adjective *lokavidū* together with the conventional formula describing the range of beings in the world as perceived by the Buddha emphasizes the special nature of this attribute.

3. In the Dvayatānupassanā Sutta occurs a passage in which the viewpoint held by the whole world (the world of beings enumerated in the conventional cosmic formulas) is contrasted with the viewpoint held by the *Ariyas*; what the whole world, deva, Māra, ascetic and brahman, etc., regard as the truth is seen by the Ariyas to be false; and vice versa (Sn p. 147).

(ii) *Legendary material.* One of the most notable passages under this heading in the Pāli canon occurs in the Sutta Nipāta, namely the Padhāna Sutta. E. Windisch, in his *Māra und Buddha*, made this sutta the starting point of his investigation of the Māra legend, for the reason that here the legend finds its finest poetical expression (*op. cit.*, p. 204). He compared the Pāli text of the Sutta with the Sanskrit version found in the Lalit-avistara, Adhy XVIII. On the basis of this comparison he was able to draw certain conclusions regarding the possible source of the highly embellished accounts of the temptation of the Buddha by Māra immediately before the Enlightenment which are found in Sanskrit versions of the life of the Buddha. The Sutta was also translated and discussed by E. J. Thomas in his *Life of the Buddha* (Ch VI). It has been subjected to a critical analysis by N. A. Jayawickrama (*University of Ceylon Review*, Vol. VIII, 1950, pp. 185 ff.).

The incident related in the present Pāli version of the Sutta, as it stands does not *manifestly* form a part of the series of events on the occasion of the Buddha's Enlightenment. The word manifestly is emphasized, in view of the possible implica-tions of the statement by E. J. Thomas, that 'the whole story of the contest with Māra is a mythological development . . . not found in the Pāli Canon. . . .' (*op cit.*, p. 74). However,

Thomas certainly concedes that the Padhāna Sutta 'contains what may be the first suggestion of the legend' (*ibid.*, p. 71).

In its present form the Sutta is a combination of two or more poems, as the Pāli commentator points out. The major portion (up to Sn 445) to which both the Mahāvastu and the Lalitavistara provide parallel versions, describes an occasion when the Buddha was striving, deep in meditation, on the bank of the Nerañjara river (the scene of the Enlightenment).[1] The Pāli text of the Sn here describes him as '*Buddha*', but the commentator points out that he was evidently not Buddha at this time, and in the Mahāvastu and Lalitavistara he is called *Bodhisattva* at this point. He is then approached by Māra, who is here called *Namuci*. The same appellation is used again at Sn 439; N. A. Jayawickrama points out that the name is a Vedic form, and indicative of an early tradition.[2] Māra speaks pitying words, commenting upon the Bodhisattva's wasted flesh and poor colour, and urges him to desist from such striving and instead to gain merit as one who lives the holy life feeding the sacrificial fire (428). Māra's approbation of Brahmanistic ritual, and of ascetic austerities is attested elsewhere in the Canon.[3] The Buddha, in reply, declares that he has not the slightest need to gain merit, and bids Māra behold in him one with serene mind, one who is wholly purified (431-435). He then proclaims his knowledge of Māra's forces (436-439). These are: desire (*kāma*), aversion (*arati*), hunger and thirst (*khuppipāsa*), craving (*taṇhā*), sloth and torpor (*thīnamiddhaṃ*), fear (*ābhirū*),[4] doubt (*vicikicchā*), self-will and cant (*makkha thamba*), gains, favours, flattery, ill-gained honours, exciting oneself and despising others. 'This, Namuci, is your army; this is Kaṇha's fighting force.' The first, second and fourth members of the list appear in personified form in the Māra-Saṃyutta as Māra's daughters, with Rāgā as a synonym for Kāma. Jayawickrama regards this personification as a 'later development' of the Māra legend. (*op. cit.*, p. 189). The Buddha's words continue: 'No coward conquers this army; but he who does gains bliss.'

In the next four verses (440-443) the idea of an approaching

[1] Majjhima-Nikāya I. 240 ff. (Mahāsaccaka Sutta).
[2] In support of this Jayawickrama quotes Neumann, '*Rede* etc.' p. 469.
[3] e.g. Mārasaṃyutta I. 1
[4] *ābhirū* is given in Dines Andersen's text, and is based on Sinhalese and Siamese MSS. The Burmese MSS. give *bhirū*.

conflict is prominent, and the passage is laden with terms connected with battle. 'See,' says the Buddha, 'I am wearing muñja grass!' The allusion here is not altogether clear; E. M. Hare points out that in the case of a brahman the wearing of a *muñja* girdle denoted a vow (*Woven Cadences*, p. 64); E. J. Thomas notes that it is a sign that the warrior intends to devote himself in battle (*Life of Buddha*, p. 73). In the *JRAS* (1930, pp. 107-8 and 897-8) the phrase is discussed; F. Otto Schrader is inclined to connect it with the idea of a *vow*, while K. Chaṭṭopādhyāya concludes that the meaning 'I gird up my loins' seems more natural. On the basis of his comparison with Lalitavistara, which, at the point where this line occurs, has '*Varaṃ mṛtyuḥ prā ṇaharo*', Windisch suggests an amended Pāli text, having as the first line of v. 440:

Varaṃ maccu pāṇaharo

He notes that the line as it stands is 'corrupt in all the Pāli MSS' (*op. cit.*, pp. 7 and 30). Although these interpretations vary in their details the general effect is to give support to the idea of an impending conflict, and this is consistent with the next words in the text: 'I would rather die in battle than live vanquished!' (*sāṅgame me mataṃ seyyo yañce jīve parājito*—Sn 440). 'Seeing Māra, ready mounted upon his elephant, and surrounded by his army (*dhajiniṃ*), I go forth to battle (*yuddhāya paccuggacchāmi*), nor will he move me from my place (*mā maṃ ṭhānā acāvayi.*—442). N. A. Jayawickrama notes that v. 442 has no parallel in the Mahāvastu, and suggests that it is therefore to be regarded as a later addition in the Pāli text. While it is true that the verse is missing from the Sanskrit versions (from the Lalitavistara as well as from the Mahāvastu), it is possible to view this omission in another light, as Windisch does in his comments at this point: 'Es folgt im Pali der 18 Sloka —*Samantā dhajiniṃ disvā*—der im Sanskrit fehlt. Ist er im Pāli zugesetzt oder im Sanskrit weggelassen? Ich vermuthe das letztere, denn er wird mehr noch als die vorausgehenden Verse *Kāmā te paṭhamā senā* u. s. w. den Anlass dazu gegeben haben, Buddha's Kampf mit Māra zu dem grotesken Bilde zu gestalten, das uns im Lalitavistara entgegentritt. Was im Padhānasutta in vollkommen durchsichtiger Weise nur bildlicher Ausdruck ist, das erscheint im Lalitavistara wörtlich genommen und zu einer mythischen Schlacht vergröbert.' (*op. cit.*, p. 29).

The text continues (443): 'That army which the world with all its devas cannot crush, against that I, by means of wisdom (*paññā*), go like a stone against an unbaked earthen bowl.'

This concludes the allusion in the Padhāna Sutta to what appears to be the Buddha's approaching battle with Māra. No actual description of the battle is given, such as may be found in the Sanskrit versions, but it is important to bear in mind what N. A. Jayawickrama has pointed out, that the narrative suttas of the Mahāvagga of the Sutta Nipāta are examples of early ballads about the Buddha's life, and that there were probably others. 'A comparison with the later BSk sources . . . shows that these three suttas (*Pabbajjā, Padhāna* and *Nālaka*) in Sn deal with only three of the numerous incidents reported in later sources. It is quite probable that some suttas parallel to those found in Lal. and Mvastu. were lost and that Sn contains only a partial picture.' (*UCR*, Vol. VI, 1948, p. 256).

Thus, there are two possible alternative views by which the Padhāna Su is regarded as testifying to the Buddha's crucial battle with Māra. In Jayawickrama's view the more explicit references to battle in the present form of the sutta, which have no parallel at that point in the BSk, e.g. Sn 440, 442, are to be regarded as later additions, under the influence of the legend of the battle as it was recounted elsewhere, i.e. in other Pāli suttas, no longer known to us, which contained the episodes which are now preserved only in the Sanskrit sources. In view of the prominence of the battle with Māra in the Sanskrit versions, this is one of the episodes with which the lost Pāli suttas may well have dealt.

On the other hand, there is the view of Windisch, that there is sufficient 'conflict' material in the Pāli version of the Padhāna to form the basis of a more extended and elaborate story of a battle with Māra, such as appears in the Sanskrit versions: Was im Padhānasutta in vollkommen durchsichtiger Weise nur bildlicher Ausdruck ist, das erscheint im Lalitavistara[1] wörtlich genommen und zu einer mythischen Schlacht vergröbert!

On either view, the conclusion is justified, that some crucial conflict with Māra is implied here in the Pāli canon. This

[1] And, it may be added, in the Mahāvastu; the existence of a somewhat corrupt version of the Padhāna Sutta within the Mvstu was not evident to Windisch until he had completed the main body of his work: see *Māra und Buddha*, p. 322.

conclusion is supported by the accounts of a crucial battle with Māra which are found in later Pāli literature (e.g. J. I. 71 f.; Sn A. 391; DhA II. 195 etc.)

After this in the Padhāna Sutta there comes a verse (444) in which the Buddha declares what he will do when the battle has been won. 'Having mastered my thought (*vasiṃkaritvā saṃkappaṃ*), and with mindfulness well established, I shall go about from kingdom to kingdom, training disciples everywhere.' (*raṭṭhā raṭṭhaṃ vicarissaṃ sāvake vinayaṃ puthu.*) The portion of the poem which is common to the Pāli version and the Lalitavistara ends half-way through this verse; instead of the words in the Pāli, *raṭṭhā raṭṭhaṃ* etc., the Sanskrit version is rounded off with the words: *Evam ukte Māraḥ pāpīyān duḥkhito durmanā anāttamanā vipratisārī tatraivāntaradhāt.* This corresponds closely to the characteristic wording with which the suttas of the Mārasaṃyutta usually end (I. 1-6; 10; II. 1-10 that is, 17 out of the first twenty suttas have this ending). Points of similarity, and contrast, between the Padhāna Sutta and the Māra suttas of the Saṃyutta Nikāya have already been considered in Ch. 3.[1] The Padhāna Sutta, like the Lalitavistara, has for its conclusion this conventional ending found also in the Saṃyutta: *tato so dummano yakkho tatth' ev' antaradhāyathā ti.* (449 cd). But between v. 444, which marks the end of the parallel with the Lalitavistara, and this concluding verse, there are found four verses which have no parallel in the Sanskrit versions (445-8). These verses, especially 446-8, are now regarded as being later than the rest of the poem (Jayawickrama, *op. cit.*, p. 109). Sn 446, beginning *Satta vassāni. . . .*' is found also in the Mārasaṃyutta, in prose form, where it stands as a heading to the 'Seven Year Sutta'. The next two verses in the Padhāna, (Sn 447-8) occur in identical form in the Seven Year Sutta.[2]

The following conclusions may now be stated:

1. The thought and ideas embodied in the major portion of the Padhāna Sutta are distinctively old; for example, the name Namuci for Māra; the allusion to Māra as a *yakkha* (449); the occurrence of three abstract qualities in the list of Māra's army (436 ff.), which *later* appear as personifications, *kāma* (=Ragā), *arati*, and *taṇhā*.

[1] See pp. 47 ff, supra.
[2] Māra-Saṃyutta, III 4.

2. The Padhāna sutta conveys the feeling of a real impending conflict, a feature which is in distinct contrast to the general tone of the suttas of the Māra-Saṃyutta.

3. No actual description of the struggle with Māra is given; this however, may have had its place in another sutta of the cycle of ballads of which, it is suggested, the Pabbajjā, the Padhāna and the Nālaka form a part. Or, alternatively the data contained in the Padhāna are sufficient to provide a good nucleus for the fuller and more elaborate accounts of the Buddha's struggle with Māra which appear in the Sanskrit sources.

4. The position of the Padhāna Sutta, among the suttas at the head of the Mahāvagga of the Sn, and immediately after the Pabbajjā Sutta, together with the mention of the River Nerañjara (Sn 425) as the scene of the episode, would appear to indicate that this is to be regarded as happening somewhere near the time of the Enlightenment. A time before the Enlightenment is assumed in the Sanskrit sources, where the central figure is referred to not as Buddha, but Bodhisattva.

Other material connected with the Māra legend to be found in the Sn is as follows.

In the Dhaniya Sutta two stanzas occur (Sn 33, 34) which are found also in the Saṃyutta Nikāya, in both the Devatā-Saṃyutta (S I. 2. 2.) and the Māra-Saṃyutta (S IV. 1. 8). In the course of a conversation between the Buddha and a rich herdsman named Dhaniya, suddenly and unannounced Māra's voice is heard, expressing the popular opinion regarding the desirability of sons:

'*Nandati puttehi puttimā etc.* . . . '

To this the Buddha replies:

'*Socati puttehi puttimā etc.* . . . '

In his critical examination of the Sutta Nipāta, N. A. Jayawickrama questions whether these stanzas belong to the original version of the Sn.[1] The appearance of Māra in this fashion in the Dhaniya Sutta thus provides no new material regarding the Māra legend, but it does serve to illustrate a tendency to introduce such references to Māra into popular ballad material of this kind, probably at a stage subsequent to the first formulation of the ballad.

[1] *op. cit.*, p. 88.

Another reference to the Māra legend may be noted at Sn 835. The Buddha, speaking to Māgandiya, is represented as referring to the occasion when the daughters of Māra came to tempt him:

Disvāna Taṇhaṃ Aratiṃ Ragañ ca
nāhosi chando api methunasmim

The Niddesa comment on this verse makes it clear that the commentator understands it as a reference to the daughters of Māra (Nd¹. 181.). Since they are clearly spoken of as persons rather than as abstract items in an allegorical list of the constituents of Māra's army (as at Sn 436), and were understood as such by the time of the composition of the Niddesa, it will be seen which way the development tended to proceed: towards personification.

(iii) *Māra: didactic material.* There are eight references to be considered under this heading: Sn 358, 733, 764, 967, 1095, 1103, 1118 f. and 1146.

Finally, there are four allusions by contemporaries of the Buddha to his conquest of Māra. He is described as a *Mārābhibhūmuni* (at 545 by Sabhiya; at 571 by Sela) and as *Mārasenappamaddana* (also by Sela at 563); at 561 the Buddha is represented as applying this epithet to himself.

1. Epithets embodying the idea of the conquest of Māra, like those supplied to the Buddha, are used also to describe the arahat. The words *abhibhuyya Mārasaṃyogaṃ* occur at Sn 733 as a description of those who are *sammaddasā vedaguno samma-d-aññāya paṇḍitā*. At Sn 1095 it is said of those who are 'mindful of perfect knowledge' (*aññāya ye satā*) that they are neither in Māra's power, nor do they wait upon Māra as servants, that is to say, do not do his will (*na te Māra-vasānugā, na te Mārassa paddhagū*).

2. In contrast to these examples are some allusions to Māra's victims. At Sn 764 those who are overcome by *bhavarāga*, who simply drift along the stream of existence, are said to be 'gone to Māra's realm' (*Māradheyyānupannā*). Sn 967 represents the Buddha as advising Sāriputta that when a bhikkhu becomes aware of 'unrest of mind' (*yad āvilattaṃ manaso vijaññā*), he should dispel it by saying: 'This belongs to Kaṇha (Māra)!' (*kaṇhassa pakkho ti vinodayeyya.*). At Sn 1103 the Buddha,

in the course of explaining the Dhamma to Bhadrāvudha, tells him that Māra has access to people by means of whatever things in the world they cling to:

yaṃ yaṃ hi lokasmiṃ upādiyanti
ten' eva Māro anveti jantuṃ.

3. Lastly, three references may be noted in which the name Maccu is used as a synonym for Māra. At Sn 357 the recently deceased Kappa is praised by his pupil Vangīsa as a true follower of the Buddha, a man who acted according as he taught, and who thus cut away the entanglement of Maccu, which is stretched out strong and is very deceiving (*Maccuno jālaṃ tataṃ māyāvino daḷhaṃ*); who saw where craving has its beginning, and thus passed beyond Māra's realm, which is so difficult to get through (*accagā vata Kappāyano Maccudheyyaṃ suduttaran ti.*).

The idea of Maccu as lord of a realm which may be transcended by him who regards the world as void, and who has uprooted all false view of self, is found at Sn 1118 f., where the Buddha is answering a question put to him by the venerable Mogharājā:

Suññato lokaṃ avekkhassu Mogharāja sadā sato
attānudiṭṭhiṃ ūhacca, evaṃ maccutaro siyā:

Of him who does this it may be said that King Maccu sees him not:

evaṃ lokaṃ avekkhantaṃ maccurājā na passati.

Similarly in Sn 1146 the Buddha declares to Piṅgiya that he by faith shall attain release, and shall reach that which is beyond Maccu's realm: '*Evam eva tvam pi pamuñcassu saddhaṃ: gamissasi tvaṃ Piṅgiya maccudheyyapāraṃ.*' The Culla Niddesa (which has the reading *maccudheyyassa pāraṃ* taking *pāraṃ* as a noun, rather than as an adverb) explains this as a reference to '*amataṃ nibbānaṃ*'. Nibbāna is thus the realm which is 'beyond' the realm where Māra reigns.

(e) *Thera- and Therīgāthā*

'There is no doubt,' wrote Wilhelm Geiger, of the Thera- and Therīgāthā, 'that these strophes contain much that belongs to the authentic Buddhist literature of the earliest times.'[1]

[1] *PLL*, p. 21.

He went on to say however, that many verses might have been the fabrication of collectors or redactors on the basis of fragmentary reminiscences. In any case, the collections, as they now exist, cannot possibly be regarded as the homogeneous work of a single intellect as R. O. Franke has suggested.

The fact that these verses represent the traditions of a *community* enhances their value for the present study: here most notably, the voices of the early disciples are heard, recounting their experiences, their temptations and their victories. It is this aspect of the Theragāthā and Therīgāthā which gives significance to the frequency with which Māra is mentioned here, and, by contrast, the very small number of references to the minor demons of popular belief. The index to Rhys David's translation of the Theragāthā shows that the references to Māra are here roughly equal in number to the references to Nibbāna. This provides a rough estimate of the prominence of Māra in this literature.[1]

The following analysis of the material will be based on the verses only, and not on the commentarial passages (included in the English translation), describing the circumstances in which the verses were spoken; if these were taken into account the Māra material would be considerably more extensive.

(i) The conventional cosmic formula in which the name of Māra occurs does not appear here. The references to Māra are fairly evenly divided between actual encounters with him, experienced by the speakers of the verses, and allusions to him in the third person. As even the verses in which Māra is addressed seldom give much hint of the circumstances of the encounter, but rather the attitude of the speaker towards the Evil One, it will be more convenient to consider all the references as of one class, since all have a fairly clear didactic intention.

The verses disclose various ways in which Māra was thought of.

These range from the picturesque and popular to the wholly abstract. The former is seen in Māra's yakkha-like characteristic of assuming various shapes and producing terrifying noises; this is attested in the words of Samiddhi addressed to

[1] The Index, of course, is based on the verses *and* the commentarial narrative. But as this holds good for both Māra and Nibbāna, it does not radically affect the approximate extent of the two terms, relative to each other.

the Evil One: '. . . make thou whatever shams thou list, thou'lt harm me not' (Thag 46). Noise as a characteristic of Māra occurs again in the words of Rāmaṇeyyaka: 'Not all the clitter clatter of your noise, . . . avail to make pulse throb and mind distraught, for one the aim to which my heart is given' (Thag 49). The idea that Māra is responsible for loud and distracting noises is no doubt related to the disturbing effect which this particular form of attack might be calculated to have on one who was engaged in meditation: Māra is plainly regarded as the opponent of meditation.

More especially however, it is the pleasure of the senses with which Māra is connected. Sense desires are a snare set by the King of Death (Thag 253). Anuruddha tells of his delicate and luxurious life at home, where he was attended by song and dance; this, he says, was 'abiding in Māra's precincts' (*Mārassa visaya*). But now, rapt in meditation, he has left behind all the objects of the senses that please and charm (Thag 893 ff.). Similarly, a woman who has adorned herself and is attended by a company of maid-servants is described as 'in brave array, like snare of Māra laid' (*alaṃkataṃ suvasanaṃ maccupāsaṃ va oḍḍitaṃ*—Thag 300; see also 268 f.; 463). This occurs several times, and on each occasion the Thera concerned tells how, analysing the sight of that which was intended to appeal to him, he realized 'the misery of it all', and his heart was set at liberty (*tato me manisikāro yoniso udapajjatha*). This meretricious quality is regarded not so much as a quality of the person thus adorned, but rather as something for which Māra is responsible: 'This is Māra's snare!' is the proper reaction. This is as true for the Sisters as it is for the Brethren. Selā, for example, speaks of the joys of sense as 'spears and javelins that pierce and rend the mortal frame'; these are not the good things of life she declares, and bids Māra begone, with his foolish suggestions: 'On every hand the love of pleasure yields. . . . Know this, O Evil One, avaunt! Here O Destroyer, thou shalt not prevail!' (Thīg 59). It is noticeable that the last few words are those which in the Māra-Saṃyutta are commonly attributed to the Buddha in his replies to Māra (*nihato tvam asi antaka*); in the same triumphant terms as the Buddha addresses the Evil One, so also do his disciples. These words are found over and over again in the Therīgāthā (59; 142; 188; 195; 203; 235), and are attributed to a number of different speakers, and may therefore be presumed to have had a common currency in the early community.

The physical body is in one place spoken of as that 'which appertains to Māra', in so far as it is a possible counter-attraction drawing the disciple away from the life of meditation (*dhir atthu pūre duggandhe, Mārapakkhe avassute*—Thag 279). Self-indulgence, in the form of lethargy, is said to open the way for Māra: Kātiyāna, overcome by sleepiness, is bidden by the Buddha not to allow Māra to overcome him thus, but rather to shake him off (Thag 411 ff.). The mind also is an instrument which may be used by the Evil One: remaining subservient to the mind (*citta*) men are subject to rebirth, for, unknowing, they are drawn along in the wake of Māra's power (*aviddasū Māravasānavattino bhavābhinandī tava citta sevakā ti*—Thag 1145). The Buddha is represented as reminding one of the Sisters of the deceptiveness of the mind, and of its attraction towards the realm of Māra (*cittena vañcitā sattā Mārassa visaye ratā*—Thīg 164). It is the way of Māra to trap his victims by unbalancing their minds by means of worldly desire (*kāma*) (Thīg 357). Besides *kāma*, the other roots of evil are also spoken of as instruments of Māra; the three roots, *rāga, dosa* and *avijjā*, are said to be Māra's bonds (Thag 281 f.), and those who have conquered these evil roots have thrown off Māra's bonds. *Avijjā*, in association with *rāga* and *dosa*, is of course, something more than intellectual ignorance, it has a moral connotation, and appears to represent the lack of real insight which accompanies and indeed underlies, passionate desire and hatred. This association of passion and moral myopia is found very frequently in the Therīgāthā in the verse which has already been mentioned: 'On every hand the love of pleasure yields, and the thick gloom of ignorance is rent;' (*sabbattha vihata nandi tamokkhandho padālito*—Thīg 59; 142; 188; 195; 203; 235.) This is bad news for Māra (*evaṃ jānāhi pāpimā*), it means that he has been 'laid low' (*nihato tvam asi antaka*).

Similarly it is said to be insight (into the true nature of things) which means the shattering of Māra's host (Thag 1095).

The conquest of Māra is equally as prominent a theme in these verses as the sense of his ubiquity and never-ceasing activity. In the most general terms the conquest of Māra is the result of yielding to the Buddha's religion; thus Abhibhūta urges his kinsmen, *yuñjatha Buddhasāsane dhunātha Maccuno senaṃ* (Thag 256). It is the Buddha pre-eminently who is the crusher of Māra's hosts (Thag 831 ff.). The first line of Vangīsa's verses in praise of the Buddha speaks of his victory over Māra (Thag 1242). The same victory is enjoyed by those who follow in the Buddha's path. In his verses describing the achievements of the enlightened ones, Moggallāna takes as his starting point the fact that they are able to conquer Māra's army: *dālemu Maccuno senaṃ ajjhattaṃ susamāhitā* (Thag 1146). This claim is repeated, with variations, in the next three verses. The claim to be able to conquer Māra is thus made prominent and emphatic. In another place the followers of the Buddha are described as *Maccuhāyino sabbe bhagavato puttā* (Thag 1236-7). Sāriputta is similarly described as *Maccuhāyina* (Thag 1177). A young bhikkhu is praised as one destined for Nibbāna, for he has defeated Māra and all his host (Thag 1166). The same words of eulogy are found in a number of places in the Therīgāthā applied to the Sisters (Thīg 7; 10; 65.). The subordination of Māra to the Arahat finds expression also in the warning which is sometimes addressed to Māra not to try to assail those who have transcended his realm: *tādisaṃ bhikkhuṃ āsajja kaṇha dukkhaṃ nigacchasīti* (Thag 25 and 1187-9).

It will be noticed that in some of the examples which have been given Maccu rather than Māra is spoken of. Apart from the commentaries, which make it clear that these two names were regarded as synonymous, the identity of the two is attested in the Theragāthā. The clearest instance of this is in v. 252 f.:

> *pañca kāmaguṇā loke sammohā pālāyiṃsu maṃ*
> *pakkhanno Māravisaye daḷhasallasamappito*
> *asakkhiṃ Maccurājassa ahaṃ pāsa pamuccituṃ* . . .

There is thus impressive evidence in the Theragāthā and Therīgāthā that the idea of Māra the Evil One was familiar to the members of the early community. Whereas their contemporaries in ancient India would regard events or phenomena calculated to inspire fear as due now to one yakkha or pisāca, now to another, to the Buddhist these were all the manifestations of the Evil One, Māra, at work. He who ruled over the realm of continued rebirth was regarded as strenuously opposed to the departure from his realm of any of his subjects. But where the Buddha and his followers were concerned, Māra was powerless. Confident in this knowledge, the Buddhist was proof against all the meretricious appeals which Māra might make.

(f) *The Jātakas*

Of special interest for the present inquiry is a passage in the Ayoghara J. The stanzas spoken by the wise Ayoghara describe the many dangers which men are likely to encounter in the course of a lifetime—armies, mad elephants, archers, snake bite, and so on; from all these dangers men can and sometimes do escape; included in this is the danger from yakkhas and pisācas and petas. But over against all these, from which escape is at least conceivable, is Maccu, death, from whom there is no escape ever. This theme forms the constant refrain of the verses:

> *Yakkhe pisāce athavāpi pete*
> *kupite pi te nijjhapanaṃ karonti*
> *na maccuno nijjhapanaṃ karonti*
> *tam me matī hoti: carāmi dhammaṃ*
>
> (— J IV. 495).

The way the inference is drawn is particularly noteworthy. The real impulse to the holy life comes from the awareness of death's inevitability; other dangers might conceivably be countered in other ways, but in the face of Maccu's grim hostility there is only one safe response: '*carāmi dhammaṃ*'. Here is seen the essential difference between the yakkhas and Māra. The yakkhas represent the many forms of danger, from which escape may be possible; they belong with that which is fortuitous, contingent, sporadic; the random ills of life which must either be endured or avoided or appeased. Maccu represents the one form of danger that is universal, all prevailing, from which escape by ordinary means is impossible; Maccu cannot be avoided, or endured, or appeased; Maccu must be met in another fashion —must be transcended, by the living of the holy life. This unitary, all embracing, universal aspect of death is also one of the outstanding features of the Buddhist symbol of Māra, and constitutes one of the basic contrasts between the Buddhist Māra-mythology and the popular yakkha-mythology.

It is, however, one of the notable features of the Jātakas that Māra appears very seldom in these stories. The few references that are found are as follows:

(i) *Legendary material* The Khadiraṅgāra J., in its 'story of the past' (*Atītavatthū*) tells how in past days the wise and good used to exercise charity and give gifts, even though threatened by Māra with hell-fire if they did so (J I. 231 ff.). A Pacceka Buddha, having fasted for seven days, asked for food at a certain mansion. At this Māra (here described as 'Lord of the realm of Kāma'—*Kāmāvacarissara Māra*), became excited, saying: 'If he gets no food he will perish. I will destroy him; I will stop the Treasurer from giving.' Māra called into being a pit of red-hot embers, eighty cubits deep, and took his stand in mid-air. The discovery of this pit by the inmates of the house caused great alarm. But the Bodhisatta (i.e. the Treasurer) said: 'Māra, the Enthraller, must have been exerting himself today to stop me from alms-giving. I have yet to learn that I am to be shaken by a hundred or a thousand Māras.' (*Ajja mayhaṃ dānantarāyaṃ kātukāmo Vasavatti Māro uyyutto bhavissati*: *na kho pana jānāmi Mārasatena Mārasahassenāpi mayhaṃ akampiyabhāvam*—J I. 232). He thereupon challenged Māra, whom he saw overhead, to say who he was. 'I am Māra,' was the reply (*Ahaṃ Māro ti*). The Bodhisatta forthwith performed a miracle, stepping on the surface of the fire, and thus succeeded in giving alms to the Pacceka Buddha. The Atītavatthū section of the Jātaka ends with the information that Māra, defeated and dejected, passed away back to his own abode (*Māro pi parājito domanassaṃ patvā attano vasanaṭṭhānam eva gato*—J I. 233).

There are some notable differences between this narrative and other legendary material already examined. The epithet here applied to Māra—*Kāmāvacarissara*—is unusual, although not out of keeping with other teaching concerning Māra; so also is the appellation Vasavattin, who elsewhere (D I. 219) appears as the chief of the Paranimmitavasavatti devas. Further, it is unlike the Māra of the Suttas to disclose his identity so readily (*Ahaṃ Māro ti*). Again, it is usual for Māra to retire discomfited and defeated, but in the Saṃyutta-Nikāya and the Suttanipāta the usual form of wording to describe this is *tato so dummano yakkho tatth' ev' antaradhāyatha*, or some slight variation, such as *dukkhī dummano tatth' ev' antaradhāyi*. In the Jātaka, however, a strikingly different form of words is used: *Māro pi parājito etc.* . . . Nevertheless the idea conveyed is the same. Thus the story of Māra found here seems to represent a different verbal tradition, but basically the same mythology.

Apart from this story there are two other references to Māra of a legendary nature. In the Suvaṇṇakakkaṭa J. the story of the crab, the Bodhisatta, the crows and the snake occurs. The black snake, who bit and poisoned the Bodhisatta, and was afterwards crushed by the crab and spiked and thrown away by the Bodhisatta, is identified as Māra. (J III. 298). In the Cullasuka J. a brahmin's failure to give alms as he should have done is explained as the result of temptation by Māra (J III. 494).

(ii) *Didactic material.* Under this heading four references are found. The Sakuṇagghi Jātaka contains the story of a quail who left his own proper ground, and was caught by a falcon, but escaped the falcon by returning to his own proper ground. As in the Saṃyutta Nikāya (S V. 146 f.), this story is told to illustrate the truth than when people leave their own proper range, Māra finds an opportunity, Māra gets a foothold. By leaving one's proper range, or venturing on to dangerous foreign ground, is meant, adds the Buddha, the five sense pleasures (*pañcakāmaguṇā*). These are then explained in detail (*cakkhuviññeyyā rūpā . . . etc.*) (J II. 60).

Similar teaching is found in the Pūtimaṃsa J. If you walk on your own proper ground, the bhikkhus are told by the Buddha, Māra will not find an entrance. The 'proper ground' is then defined as consisting of the four meditations, the holy eightfold path, and the nine transcendental conditions: *etasmiṃ hi vo gocare carataṃ na lacchati Māro otāraṃ* (J III. 532).

Jātaka 536 contains a reference to Māra under the name of Namuci. A man of insight, it is said, avoids the snare laid by Namuci (*Namucipāsavākaraṃ*) (J V. 453). In Jātaka 514 reference is made to Māra as the holder of a position in the universe which, it is implied, is an exalted one, ranking with Sakka and Brahmā (*Sakkatta-Māratta-Brahmādiṃ*—J V. 53).

Thus in only two of these four references is it strictly true to speak of teaching connected with Māra, for the last two are only brief incidental references.

Such, legendary and didactic together, are the seven passages in the five hundred and fifty Jātakas in which any reference is made to Māra. The reference to yakkhas and rakkhasas are, on the other hand, considerably more numerous, and it must be noted that this proportion between the Māra-mythology and the yakkha mythology is in marked contrast to what has been observed elsewhere in the Canon. What Māra-mythology there is, is basically the same kind as in the Suttas, but here it is very little in evidence.

(g) *Remaining books*

The descriptive survey of the demonology of the Sutta Piṭaka is now complete, and the ground has been covered, but for a few isolated references in the books of the Khuddaka Nikāya which have not so far been mentioned, but can be dealt with briefly.

There are some allusions to Māra in the *Niddesa*, but these arise out of the references in the Sutta Nipāta, upon which the Niddesa is a commentary, and in so far as the Niddesa references contribute to our understanding of the subject they have already been taken into account. They have some minor value in providing short compendiums on the subject of Māra, since they consist usually of lists of synonyms for Māra (for example; *Māro ti yo so Māro Kaṇho Adhipati Antagū Namuci Pamattabandhu*—Nd² on Sn 1095), or lists of Māra's devices (*Māra-pāsañ ca='balisañ ca; 'āmissañ ca: 'visayañ ca: 'nivāsañ ca: 'gocarañ ca: 'bandhanañ ca*—Nd² *ibid.*).

The *Buddhavaṃsa* provides in one passage confirmation of the tradition which spoke of the Buddha's conquest of Māra as one of his outstanding attributes:

> *Mārasenam pamadditvā patto sambodhiṃ uttamaṃ*
> *dhammacakkaṃ pavattesi anukampāya pāṇinam* (B 54).

These words occur in connexion with Sikkhi, the twentieth Buddha, and it is worthy of note that in the case of other Buddhas, parallel statements occur at corresponding points in the narratives; thus, other Buddhas are spoken of as shattering all ignorance (*avijjaṃ sabbam padāletvā*—B 52), or conquering the thirst and fires of passion (*rāgāggitaṇhānaṃ vijjitaṃ*—B 56) or destroying all darkness (*nihantvāna tamaṃ sabbaṃ*—chs. 4, 14, 16, 17, 18.). The opposition which a Buddha has to overcome is thus an essential feature of the Buddha-legend as it had developed by the time of the 'composition' of the Buddhavaṃsa; this antagonism may be expressed in a variety of ways, among which is the idea of Māra, who is crushed by the Buddha.

6 VINAYA PIṬAKA

(i) *Conventional formulas.*

The cosmic formula, describing 'this world, with its devas, its Māra, its Brahmā etc.' occurs a number of times. In most instances this is the usual attribution to the Buddha of the power to discern the entire world with all its constituent beings: ('*nāhaṃ taṃ passāmi sadevake loke samārake sabrahmake* etc. . . .' —I. 225; see also Vin III 1 f.; III. 90; I. 11). In the Mahāvagga the connexion between the condition of Enlightenment and the supernatural insight which sees the world in this way is emphasized. 'So long as the vision of knowledge of these four Ariyan truths was not well purified by me, so long was I not thoroughly awakened to the world with its devas, its Māra etc. . . . But when . . . (this vision of knowledge was well purified), then I was thoroughly awakened to this world with its devas, its Māra etc. . . .' (*n'eva tāvāhaṃ sadevake loke samārake* (*etc.*) *anuttaram sammāsambodhiṃ abhisambuddho . . . yato ca kho me bhikkhave imesu catusu ariyasaccesu . . . suvisuddhaṃ ahosi athāhaṃ bhikkhave sadevake loke samārake . . . sammāsambodhiṃ abhisambuddho ti paccaññāsim.*—Vin I. 11). Only he who is Awakened, or Enlightened, can fully discern the world and its constituent beings, including Māra.

(ii) *Legendary material*

In the account of the Buddha's Enlightenment given in the Mahāvagga it is related how, during the last watch of the night, he rehearsed the *paṭicca samuppāda* series, in direct and reverse order, and then, having understood the matter thus, it is said he uttered the following lines:

> Truly when things grow plain to the ardent meditating brahman,
> Routing the host of Māra does he stand, like the sun that illuminates the sky.
> (*Yadā have pātubhavanti dhammā ātāpino jhāyato brāhmaṇassa*
> *vidhūpayaṃ tiṭṭhati Mārasenaṃ suriyo va obhāsayaṃ antalikkhan ti.*—Vin I. 2).

The Mahāvagga contains also a sutta which has already been encountered in the Saṃyutta Nikāya (*Mārasaṃyutta*, I. 5:

Pāsa). In this Māra speaks of the 'snare' with which he declares the Buddha is still bound. To it is here added another gātha, also from the Saṃyutta (Mārasaṃyutta II. 5: *Mānasam*), in which Māra now declares that he will bind the Buddha with the snare of the mind (*manas*). In both gāthas Māra's utterance ends: 'Recluse, you will not get free from me!' (*na me samaṇa mokkhasīti*). In both of his replies to Māra the Buddha concludes his refutation of Māra with the words, 'Humbled art thou, Destroyer!' (*nihato tvam asi Antakā ti*). The sutta ends with the stylized form of ending found in the Māra-saṃyutta: *atha kho Mārā pāpimā 'jānāti maṃ bhagavā, jānāti maṃ sugato,' ti dukkhī dummano tatth' ev' antaradhāyīti*. (Vin I. 21).

The duplication of this material, in the Saṃyutta Nikāya and the Vinaya, is in itself a further indication of the fairly commonplace nature of the Māra theme.

Another similar example of repetition is found in the reference by Ānanda to the reason why he had failed to ask the Buddha to remain alive for a full life-span. 'But I, honoured sirs, because my mind was obsessed with Māra, did not ask the Lord saying, "Let the Lord remain for a (full) life-span. . . . "[1]' The fact that this incident of the 'possession' of Ānanda by Māra is part of the very important Mahāparinibbāna Sutta would sufficiently guarantee its prominence in the tradition. From another point of view it may be said that the fact that such references to the presence and the activities of Māra are included in a sutta of such primary importance is a good indication of the fairly prominent role accorded to Māra in the orthodox tradition.

(iii) *Didactic material*

Under this heading comes one reference of special interest as it is one which represents Māra as the head of an assembly or faction (*kāya*). This is in the Suttavibhaṅga, where reference is made to 'a certain devatā of the assembly of Māra, (*aññatarā Mārakāyikā devatā*) (Vin III. 69). The commentary declares that this was 'not a well-known earth-devatā, a holder of false views, on the side of Māra, taking Māra's part.' (VA. 400).

One final point which remains to be made with regard to the Māra theme is that it may well underlie a considerable amount of the material in the Vinaya without specific reference to Māra

[1] Vin II, 289.

being made. The particular section of the Vinaya of which this may be true is that which is called *Pārājika* (Sutta Vibhaṅga). It is the title which suggests this possibility. Commenting on the word *pārājika*, the editors of *Vinaya Texts* (SBE Vol. 13) say: 'This may mean specifically defeat in the struggle with Māra the Evil One; but more probably defeat in the struggle against evil generally, defeat in the effort to accomplish the object for which the Bhikkhu entered the Order, in the effort to reach the 'supreme goal' of Arahatship'.[1] It is scarcely necessary to differentiate between Māra the Evil One and 'evil generally'. Nothing could be more general than the range of function ascribed to Māra in the Suttas; nothing more comprehensive than his identification with the five *khandhas*. It is scarcely necessary to ask whose, according to the Suttas, is the advantage when a bhikkhu fails to accomplish the object for which he entered the Order, or by whom he has been defeated. The whole range of references to Māra in the Canon leave no doubt on this subject.

Moreover, from the use of the word *pārājika* (the generally accepted etymology of which involves the idea of 'defeat'—assumed by Rhys Davids and Oldenberg in their above-quoted comment) it is evident that the existence of some kind of antagonism to the holy life is implied; this may be personal or impersonal. Now it has already been noted that the symbol of Māra itself covers a whole range of meaning, from the picturesque notion of the yakkha, to the impersonal conception of Māra revealed in the Buddha's words to Rādha (S III. 188 f.).

There is thus probably to be found here, in the use of this title *pārājika*, a implicit reminder to the bhikkhus for whom these regulations were made, that they are engaged in a conflict; there is the sense of opposition to be encountered and therefore there is the possibility of defeat. That the bhikkhu's life *was* thought of in this way is already clear from the description of it in these terms in the Itivuttaka (It 75; see supra p. 143). Whatever may have been the root-meaning of the word *pārājika*[2] the fact that Buddhaghosa interprets it as 'suffering defeat' appears to support the suggestion made above that there was a tradition among early Buddhists of speaking and thinking in

[1] Op. cit., p. 3.

[2] On the derivations that have been suggested, see E. J. Thomas, *History of Buddhist Thought*, p. 16, n. 2.

terms of a spiritual antagonism to the life of holiness, a tradition which, earlier or later, had, by Buddhaghosa's time, attached itself to the word *pārājika*.

7 ABHIDHAMMA-PITAKA

References to demons and to Māra are alike very few in the Abhidhamma-Piṭaka. In the first book, the *Dhammasaṇganī*, among a long list of synonyms for greed there occur the three terms 'Māra's trap, Māra's fish-hook, Māra's domain' (*Mārapaso, Mārabalisam, Māravisayo*—Dhs 1059, repeated at 1136). The conventional cosmic formula, concerning this world 'with its devas, its Māra, its Brahmā etc. . . .', occurs in the fourth book, the *Puggalapaññatti* (PTS edn. p. 57). In the fifth book, the *Kathā-vatthu*, Māra is mentioned in order to give the circumstances in which some verses were spoken by the bhikkhunī Vajirā: they were her reply to Māra's false speculations about Being (*satta*). (KV 66. See also sutta 10 of the Bhikkhunī-Saṃyutta, and the Mahāniddesa on Sn 951). There is mention also in this book of the 'devas of the Māra group', who are said to convey impurity to an Arahat, with the intention of causing doubt as to his attainment (II. 1. 3). The cosmic formula, including Māra, is found here also (KV 457). There are some references to *asuras*, since these constitute one of the four evil forms of rebirth that are possible to men, and which are dealt with in the course of Abhidhamma discussions.

In comparison with the vast compass of the whole Abhidhamma-Piṭaka, such references are less than slight, and the Abhidhamma-piṭaka has to be examined, if it is to be examined at all in this connexion, in respect of its virtual neglect or omission of the mythological categories of the kind which occur in such abundance in the Sutta-piṭaka.

BIBLIOGRAPHY

1. *Pāli Texts used*

Vinaya Piṭaka:

Vol. I: Mahāvagga, ed. by H. Oldenberg (London 1879).
Vol. II: Cullavagga, ed. by H. Oldenberg (London 1880).
Vol. III: Sutta vibhaṅga, Pt. I, ed. by H. Oldenberg (London 1881).
Vol. IV: Sutta vibhaṅga, Pt. II, ed, by H. Oldenberg (London 1882).
Vol. V: Parivāra, ed. by H. Oldenberg (London 1883)

Sutta Piṭaka:

Dīgha Nikāya Vols. I-III, ed. by T. W. Rhys Davids & J. E. Carpenter (London 1890–1911).
Majjhima Nikāya, Vol. I, ed. by V. Trenckner (London 1888).
Majjhima Nikāya, Vol. II, ed. by Lord Chalmers (London 1898).
Majjhima Nikāya, Vol. III, ed. by Lord Chalmers (London 1899).
Aṅguttara Nikāya, Vol. I, ed. by R. Morris (London 1885).
Aṅguttara Nikāya, Vol. II, ed. by R. Morris (London 1888).
Aṅguttara Nikāya, Vol. III, ed. by E. Hardy (London 1896).
Aṅguttara Nikāya, Vol. IV, ed. by E. Hardy (London 1899).
Aṅguttara Nikāya, Vol. V, ed. by E. Hardy (London 1900).
Saṃyutta Nikāya, Vol. I, ed. by M. L. Feer (London 1884).
Saṃyutta Nikāya, Vol. II, ed. by M. L. Feer (London 1888).
Saṃyutta Nikāya, Vol. III, ed. by M. L. Feer (London 1890).
Saṃyutta Nikāya, Vol. IV, ed. by M. L. Feer (London 1894).
Saṃyutta Nikāya, Vol. V, ed. by M. L. Feer (London 1898).

Khuddaka Nikāya:

Dhammapada, ed. by Sūriyagoda Sumangala Thera (London 1914).
Udānam, ed. by P. Steinthal (London 1885).
Itivuttaka, ed. by E. Windisch (London 1889).
Sutta Nipāta, ed. by Dines Andersen & Helmer Smith (London 1913).
Thera/Therīgāthā, ed. by H. Oldenberg and R. Pischel (London 1930).
Jātaka (6 vols.), ed. by V. Fausböll (London 1877-96).
Mahāniddesa (2 vols.), ed. by L. de la Vallée Poussin and E. J. Thomas (London 1916-17).
Cullaniddesa, ed. by W. Stede (London 1918).

Buddhavaṃsa, ed. by R. Morris (London 1882).
Cariyāpiṭaka, ed. by R. Morris (London 1882).

Abhidhamma Piṭaka:

Dhammasaṅganī, ed. by E. Müller (London 1885).
Vibhaṅga, ed. by C. A. F. Rhys Davids (London 1904).
Kathāvatthu, ed. by A. C. Taylor (London 1894).
Puggalapaññatti, ed. by R. Morris (London 1883).
Dhātukathā, ed. E. R. Gooneratne (London 1892).
Yamaka (2 vols), ed. by C. A. F. Rhys-Davids (London 1911-13).
Paṭṭhāna, ed. by C. A. F. Rhys-Davids (London 1906)

Abhidhammattha-saṅgaha, ed. by Dharmānanda Kosambī (Ahmadabad 1922).

2. *Translations*

The Book of the Discipline (Vinaya-Piṭaka), by I. B. Horner, (5 vols. London, 1940–52).

The Dialogues of the Buddha (Dīgha-Nikāya), by T. W. Rhys Davids (3 vols. London, 1899-1921).

Middle Length Sayings (Majjhima-Nikāya), by I. B. Horner (3 vols. London, 1954-9).

Gradual Sayings, (Aṅguttara-Nikāya), by F. L. Woodward and E. M. Hare, (5 vols, London, 1932-6).

Kindred Sayings (Saṃyutta-Nikāya), by C. A. F. Rhys Davids and F. L. Woodward (5 vols, London, 1917-30).

The Dhammapada, by S. Radhakrishnan (London, 1950).

The Dhammapada, by Nārada Thera (London, 1954).

Minor Anthologies of the Pāli Canon Vol. 2 (Udāna and Itivuttaka), by F. L. Woodward (London, 1935).

Woven Cadences (Sutta Nipāta), by E. M. Hare (London, 1945).

Psalms of the Early Buddhists: *Psalms of the Brethren* (Theragāthā) (1913) and *Psalms of the Sisters* (Therīgāthā) (1909), by C. A. F. Rhys Davids.

The Jātaka, translated under the editorship of E. B. Cowell (6 vols. Cambridge, 1895-1913).

A Compendium of Philosophy (Abhidhammattha-Saṅgaha), by S. Z. Aung and C. A. F. Rhys Davids (London, 1910).

The Abhidhammattha-Saṅgaha Part I, by Nārada Thera (Colombo 1947).

The Buddhacarita, by E. H. Johnston (1936).

The Mahāvastu, by J. J. Jones (3 Vols. London, 1949-56).

Buddhist Texts through the Ages, ed. E. Conze (Oxford, 1954).

Buddhist Scriptures, by E. Conze (Penguin Classics, London 1959).

3. *Language and literature*

W. Geiger: *Pāli literature and language* (Calcutta, 1956).
B. C. Law: *History of Pāli Literature,* Vol. I. (London, 1933).
N. A. Jayawickrama: 'Various critical studies of the Sutta Nipāta', in *University of Ceylon Review,* Vol. VIII 1950, etc.
S. Z. Aung: Abhidhamma Literature in Burma, in *JPTS.* 1910-12.
M. H. Bode: *Pāli Literature in Burma* (London, 1909).
The Pāli Text Society's *Pāli-English Dictionary* (London, 1925).
F. Edgerton: *Buddhist Hybrid Sanskrit Dictionary* (Yale, 1953).

4. *Indian and Buddhist Mythology*

Bloomfield, M., *Hymns of the Atharva-Veda* (SBE, Vol. 42).
Hopkins, E. W., *Epic Mythology* (Strasbourg, 1915).
Masson, J., *La Religion Populaire dans le Canon Bouddhique Pāli* (Louvain, 1942).
Macdonell, A. A., *Vedic Mythology* (Strasbourg, 1897).
Windisch, E., *Māra und Buddha* (Leipzig, 1895).
Whitney, W. D., *The Atharva-Veda, translation and notes,* Harvard Oriental Series Vols. 7 and 8 (Cambridge, Mass, 1905).

5. *Buddhist Doctrine*

Dasgupta, S. *A History of Indian Philosophy,* Vol. I. (Chap. 5) (Cam., 1957).
McGovern, W. M., *Buddhist Philosophy, I. Cosmology* (1923).
Murti, T. R. V., *The Central Philosophy of Buddhism* (Calcutta, Allen & Unwin, 1955).
Nyanaponika, Thera, *Abhidhamma Studies* (Colombo, 1949).
Nyanatiloka, Mahāthera, *Buddhist Dictionary* (Colombo, 1950) *Guide Through the Abhidhamma-piṭaka* (Colombo, 1957).
Stcherbatsky, Th., *The Central Conception of Buddhism* (London, 1923).
Thomas, E. J., *History of Buddhist Thought* (London 1933).
de la Vallée Poussin L., *Théorie des douzes causes* (1913)

6. *Buddhism as a Religion*

Bigandet, P., *The Life or Legend of Gaudama, The Buddha of the Burmese* (2nd Ed., Rangoon, 1866).
Hackman, H., *Buddhism as a Religion* (London, 1910).
Hall, H. F., *The Soul of a People* (4th Ed. London, 1902),
Lamotte, E., *Histoire du Bouddhisme Indien* (Louvain, 1958).
Mendelson, E. M., Religion and Authority in Modern Burma, (*The World Today* March 1960).
Pratt, J. B., *The Pilgrimage of Buddhism* (New York, 1928).

Ray, N. R., *Theravāda Buddhism in Burma* (Calcutta, 1946).
Scott, Sir J. G., *The Burman: His Life and Notions* (2 vols. London, 1882).
Slater, R. H., *Paradox and Nirvana* (Chicago 1951).
Thomas, E. J., *The Life of Buddha as Legend and History* (London, 1927).
Tilbe, H. H., *Pāli Buddhism* (Rangoon, 1900).

7. *General Works*
Bapat, P. V., (ed) *2500 Years of Buddhism* (Govt. of India, 1956).
Eliot, Sir C., *Hinduism and Buddhism*, (3 vols. London, 1921).
Rhys Davids, T. W., *Buddhist India* (London, 1903).
Sangarakshita, Bhikkhu, *A Survey of Buddhism* (2nd Edn., Bangalore, 1959).

ABBREVIATIONS USED

A	When appended to another abbreviation, indicates the Pāli commentary to that work (e.g. DA=Buddhaghosa's commentary of the Dīgha-Nikāya).
A	Aṅguttara-Nikāya.
AbhS	Abhidhammattha-saṇgaha.
AV	Atharva Veda.
B	Buddhavaṃsa.
BD	Buddhist Dictionary, by Nyanatiloka (Colombo, 1950).
D	Dīgha-Nikāya.
Dhp	Dhammapada.
ERE	Encyclopaedia of Religion & Ethics.
GS	Gradual Sayings, a translation of the Aṅguttara Nikāya, by F. L. Woodward & E. M. Hare (5 vols. London, 1932-1936).
HB	Hinduism and Buddhism, by Sir Charles Eliot (3 vols. London, 1921).
IHQ	Indian Historical Quarterly.
It	Itivuttaka.
J	Jātaka.
JPTS	Journal of the Pāli Text Society.
JRAS	Journal of the Royal Asiatic Society.
JSS	Journal of the Siam Society.
KS	Kindred Sayings, a translation of the Saṃyutta Nikāya, by C. A. F. Rhys Davids & F. L. Woodward (5 vols. London 1917-30).

LLG	The Life or Legend of Gaudama, the Buddha of the Burmese: P. Bigandet (2nd Edition. Rangoon, 1866).
M	Majjhima-Nikāya.
MS	Middle Length Sayings, a translation of the Majjhima-Nikāya, by I. B. Horner (3 vols. London, 1954-9).
MV	Mahāvastu.
N	Nikāya.
PED	The Pāli Text Society's Pāli-English Dictionary, ed. by T. W. Rhys-Davids & W. Stede (1925).
PLL	Pāli Literature and Language, by W. Geiger (2nd Edn. Calcutta, 1956).
PTS	Pāli Text Society.
S	Saṃyutta Nikāya.
SBE	Sacred Books of the East.
Sn	Sutta Nipāta.
Su	Sutta
Thag	Theragāthā.
ThBB	Theravadā Buddhism in Burma, by N. R. Ray (Calcutta, 1946).
Thīg	Therīgāthā.
UCR	University of Ceylon Review.
Ud	Udānaṃ.
Vin	Vinaya.
Vis	Visuddhi-magga.

References to the Pāli Text are usually made by citing the book (and, if necessary, the volume), and the page number, and this in most cases the edition of the Pāli Text Society. In the case of the Sutta Nipāta, the Theragāthā and the Therīgāthā, however, the numbers refer to the verse, not to the page.

I. GENERAL INDEX

Abhidhamma, 31–41, 77, 130, 163
Abhidhamma-piṭaka, 73, 130, 163
Abhidhammattha-saṇgaha, 32–6
abhiññā, 68, 96, 101, 110, 116, 141, 144
ABRAHAM, 93
adhipateyyā, 113
Adhipati, 55
Agañña Su, 97
agape, 84
agati, 107
Ahriman, 46
Ajakalāpa, 28
Ākoṭaka, 130
Āḷavikā, 129
Anāgami, the, 59
Ānanda, 50, 99, 110, 111, 139, 161
Āṇañjasappāya Su, 109
ANAWRAHTA, King of Burma, 72
Anglo-German school, 49
Aṇguttara-Nikāya, 23, 24, 83, 110–16
Animism, in Burma, 12 ff.
in S.E. Asia, 20 f., 78 f.
characteristic attitude of, 26–8, 40 f., 67, 78 f.
Antaka, 55, 57, 65, 70, 118, 120
apāya, 22, 24, 143
Apocalyptic literature, Jewish, 82
Applications of mindfulness, 64, 135 f.
Arahat, 36, 49 f., 52, 59, 78, 106, 113, 116, 126, 155, 162 f.
Arati, 127, 148, 150
archai, 113
Ariyapariyesana Su, 108
Arūpaloka: see next
Arūpāvacara, 32, 33, 59, 124
āsavas, 127, 142
Asuras, 21–6, 33, 83, 98, 112, 115, 135, 143, 163
asurinda, 21, 23, 113
Atharva Veda, 15 f., 19, 24, 25, 56
ātman, 38
Āṭānatiya rukkham, 98
Su, 104
AUNG, S.Z., 33, 42
Austerities, 122, 127, 130
avijjā, 36 (avidyā) 39, 51, 60, 61, 79, 106, 114, 126, 154
Avassuto Su, 134
āyatanas, 36 f.
Āyu Su, 123

Bahudhātaka Su, 101
Baka, the Brahmā, 51, 61, 101 f.
Bālisiko Su, 135
Bangkok, 75
Bhadrāvudha, 151
Bhāradvāja, 143
bhavaṇga, 67
bhaya, 88
Bhikkhus, 50, 51, 63, 64, 72, 75, 77, 100, 103, 106, 108, 109 f., 114, 116 f., 118 ff., 131, 140, 143, 150
Bhikkhu-saṃyutta, 74
Bhikkhunīs, 51, 60, 79, **117**, 129 f., 163
Bhikkhunī-saṃyutta, 43, 47, 51, 52, 74, 80, 117, 128 ff., 163
bhūta-vijjā, 19
bhūtapubbaṃ, 29
BLOOMFIELD, M., 18
Bodhisatta, 54, 97, 145, 149
Bojjhaṇgā, 63 f., 135
Bojjhaṇga-saṃyutta, 71, 135
BOUQUET, A. C., 13
Brahmā, 96, 101, 138
Brahman householders, 121
farmer, 143
Brahmanism, 18 f., 26 f., 56, 65, 76, 145
Brahmanimantanika Su, 43, 51, 60, 101
Bṛhadāraṇyaka Upaniṣad, 56
BUDDHA, The, able to recognize Māra, 50, 75, 102, 121
as Boddhisatta, 54
as solar myth, 48
as 'world-knower' (*lokavidu*), 49 f., 96, 100 f., 109, 110, 116, 139, 141, 143 f., 163
conquest of Māra, 47, 48, 50, 53, 60, 62, 74, 79, 84, 150
crusher of Māra's hosts, 98
encounters with Māra, 58, 99, 101 f., 105 f., 118–28, 144–9, 160 f.
Enlightenment of, 47, 49, 53, 105 f., 110, 116, 144, 149, 160

II. INDEX OF REFERENCES TO THE PĀLI CANON

INDEX II